Forever Free

Answering Your Questions on Deliverance, Demonic Strategies, and the Spirit Realm

Forever Free

Dr. Kevin L. Zadai

© 2024 Kevin L. Zadai.

All rights reserved. This book is protected by the copyright laws of the United States of America. This book may not be copied or reprinted for commercial gain or profit. The use of short quotations or the copying of an occasional page for personal or group study is permitted and encouraged. Permission will be granted upon request.

Unless otherwise indicated, Scripture quotations are taken from the New King James Version. Copyright © 1982 by Thomas Nelson, Inc. Used by permission. All rights reserved.

Scripture quotations marked (NLT) are taken from the Holy Bible, New Living Translation, copyright ©1996, 2004, 2015 by Tyndale House Foundation. Used by permission of Tyndale House Publishers, a Division of Tyndale House Ministries, Carol Stream, Illinois 60188. All rights reserved.

Scripture quotations marked (TPT) are from The Passion Translation®. Copyright © 2017, 2018 by Passion & Fire Ministries, Inc. Used by permission. All rights reserved. www.thePassionTranslation.com.

Scripture quotations marked (ESV) are from the ESV® Bible (The Holy Bible, English Standard Version®), copyright © 2001 by Crossway, a publishing ministry of Good News Publishers. Used by permission. All rights reserved.

Scripture quotations marked (MSG) are taken from The Message, copyright © 1993, 2002, 2018 by Eugene H. Peterson. Used by permission of NavPress. All rights reserved. Represented by Tyndale House Publishers, Inc.

Please note that Warrior Notes publishing style capitalizes certain pronouns in Scripture that refer to the Father, Son, and Holy Spirit, which may differ from some publishers' styles. Take note that the name "satan" and related names are not capitalized. We choose not to acknowledge him, even to the point of violating accepted grammatical rules. The author and Warrior Notes have made an intentional decision to italicize many Scriptures in block quotes.

Warrior Notes Publishing
P O Box 1288
Destrehan, LA 70047

Cover design: Virtually Possible Designs

For more information about our school, go to www.warriornotesschool.com.
Reach us on the internet: www.Kevinzadai.com

ISBN 13 TP: 978-1-6631-0109-9

ISBN 13 eBook: 978-1-6631-0110-5

ISBN 13 Audiobook: 978-1-6631-0111-2

Dedication

I dedicate this book to the Lord Jesus Christ. When I died during surgery and met with Jesus on the other side, He insisted that I return to life on earth and that I help people with their destinies. Because of Jesus's love and concern for people, the Lord has actually chosen to send a person back from death to help everyone who will receive that help so that their destiny and purpose are secure in Him.

I want You, Lord, to know that when You come to take me to be with You someday, I sincerely hope that people don't remember me but remember the revelation of Jesus Christ that You have shown through me. I want others to know that I am merely being obedient to my heavenly calling and mission, which is to reveal Your plan for the fulfillment of the divine destiny for each of God's children.

Acknowledgments

In addition to sharing my story with everyone through the book *Heavenly Visitation: A Guide to the Supernatural,* God has commissioned me to write over eighty books and study guides. Most recently, the Lord gave me the commission to release this book, *Forever Free*. I want to thank everyone who has encouraged me, assisted me, and prayed for me during the writing of this work. Special thanks to my wonderful wife, Kathi, for her love and dedication to the Lord and me. Thank you to my excellent staff for the wonderful job editing this book.

Contents

Introduction

The Father's heartbeat for the body of Christ at this time is that they arise to their fullest potential in Christ, unhindered by influences of trauma, rejection, and oppressive spirits. My wife, Kathi, and I, through much prayer and fasting, will give you keys to be forever free in your relationships and walk with the Lord.

You will embark on a journey of discovery about deliverance and how the devil uses a lack of understanding to cause issues and entrap people. Every single one of us needs deliverance in some way.

I want to pray over this book:

> Thank You, Heavenly Father, and thank You, Jesus, who has been given the name above all names. You are the supreme ruler of the universe. Everything You say overrules any government on this earth. Thank You for Your justice coming forth from the cross.

> Thank You for speaking to the Father on our behalf—we are forgiven. Thank You for the books written about us before we were born. These books are sealed and sure. Thank You, Lord God, for letting us worship You and allowing us to take back our country. Amen.

Throughout this book, you will find prayers to help you become forever free. I encourage you to speak these prayers verbally to release the power of the Holy Spirit in the areas where you need deliverance.

The Lord desires to speak to us so we don't have to be deceived and to understand how we can be free forever. The Lord's presence and the move of God are among us. You want to hear that who the Son sets free is indeed free (John 8:36). When the Holy Spirit speaks through you, He will speak from the Father because Jesus already said it. The Holy Spirit was sent to take the place of Jesus on earth.

Jesus said that He was only speaking what His Father was saying and doing (John 12:49–50). Then He said that another one (the Holy Spirit) like Him would come and do the same thing. The Holy Spirit would not speak on His own, but when He speaks, He reminds us of what Jesus said (John 14). Jesus told us this would happen; the Holy Spirit would lead us into all truth (John 16:13). This is because He is the Spirit of truth. The Holy Spirit is an advocate. He will only say what Jesus and the Father have already said.

You're only responsible for what you have received from Jesus and the Father. The Holy Spirit will not say anything contrary to what has been spoken. He's only going to enforce the documents that are written already. You have a record in Heaven written about you.

> *You've gone into my future to prepare the way, and in kindness you follow behind me to spare me from the harm of my past. You have laid your hand on me!.*
>
> **—Psalm 139:5 TPT**

He's already in your future.

> *You saw who you created me to be before I became me! Before I'd ever seen the light of day, the number of days you planned for me were already recorded in your book.*
>
> **—Psalm 139:16 TPT**

The Holy Spirit will express what the Father is saying and remind us of what Jesus said. He's going to talk about the future and call the things that are not as though they are. Prophetic words must be expressed so they can be activated by faith in a person's spirit. If they are not activated by faith, we end up just like Jesus did in His hometown. He couldn't even heal the sick there because the people didn't discern who He was; they only knew Him as the son of a carpenter. To them, He was not the Son of God or the Messiah but the guy who lived down the street that built tables and chairs. According to the Bible, He couldn't do any miracles except heal people with a few minor ailments.

The people's faith or lack thereof hindered the Son of God from doing the Father's will because God went around doing good through Jesus and healing everyone oppressed by the devil. His intention was to never make anyone sick. The Spirit and the Father were working with Jesus.

As I mentioned, Jesus then went to the Father and sent the Holy Spirit. Our tongue is a rudder steering the whole ship, and what you say with your mouth, if you believe with your heart, shall be done. Jesus said that if you speak to a mountain, it shall be removed if you believe in your heart and not your head.

You can't fail when your spirit is aligned with the Holy Spirit. You are a conduit and speak according to what God is saying and can't stop what God is doing. You are not helping God but yielding to Him, which prevents familiar spirits from working.

God invests in you and puts the Holy Spirit in you. As you learn how to yield and surrender to Him, then insights from the other realm and the future come out of your mouth. You can prevent familiar spirits from working in your life. Familiar spirits are those that have been assigned to your bloodline. You should see how these familiar spirits get all upset when you start revealing all the secrets; they will begin to threaten you. The Holy Spirit always speaks the truth and leads you into the truth.

You could be sick right now; that's a fact, but it's not the truth. The absolute truth is found in the Word of God, and Peter said by His stripes we were healed (1 Peter 2:24). Also, Revelation says that the Lamb was slain before the foundation of the world (Revelation 13:8). Jesus was slain before we were even born, so we're already healed.

You have already made it into your future. Most importantly, everything about the Holy Spirit and the Word of God is truth.

Jesus consistently addressed unbelief, and why they did not receive due to their lack of faith. If I confront people about their unbelief and tell them this is why they are not receiving, they will ask why I am so judgmental. You are responsible for judging yourself. The Holy Spirit comes with truth, not facts. He will seem in your face at times because He's going to take you right to the wall, and He won't put up with any shenanigans.

A Christian cannot be possessed but can be hijacked through inaccurate data. The demons can control your ears and eyes and feed you erroneous information. They can control your feelings and provide false information to get you off course, to steer you off track. If an evil spirit isn't successful in deceiving you, they will find someone they can affect.

As a Christian, you need to allow the Holy Spirit to enforce the covenant and lead you by speaking the words from His heart, which are truth and not facts. You call the things that are not as though they were, and then the lion will seek to devour you but cannot (1 Peter 5:8). If he can't devour you, he seeks someone else; this is how you get rid of familiar spirits.

Children will throw a fit if you don't give them attention, and they don't care if it's negative or positive. People who operate in rejection are driven by emotions, so they want attention and don't feel valued. These folks need to be the center of attention because they feel rejected. If people are needy, give them space because at times we're all needy. We must mature so that we're outwardly giving instead of always needy and receiving. We must become a distribution center.

See, the Holy Spirit wants to use us and move through us with all the provision of God in every area. However, I'm not waiting for someone to give anything to me. God has called me to be a distribution center. I'm not waiting for money because we're not in debt. And I won't start crying while I take an offering because I'm a distribution center. The body of Christ needs to come to the point of maturity and stop needing attention.

> **The Holy Spirit wants to use us and move through us with all the provision of God in every area.**

Evil spirits are rejected and locked out because there is no redemption for them; no matter what they do, they will never be redeemed. The devil and demons will be thrown into the lake of fire, but they're roaming the earth now.

Unclean spirits understand you because they were like you at one time. Unlike you, they have no redemption or chance of returning; therefore, they hate you. They will do everything they can to destroy God and you because they have nothing and can't win. When a person is like that, it's just vengeance and torment. The whole idea is that evil spirits are operating through rejection.

If you want to eliminate familiar spirits, do not give their words any power or even acknowledge them. The mode of operation of a familiar spirit is to get you to respond by acting wrongly. Before you know it, they are driving you to make you believe this is the way you are, and it will always be this way. You find yourself in a vicious cycle where someone is always doing the same thing to you, and you say that this always happens to me.

When you do that, you've just agreed with that familiar spirit, and now he brings his friends along. Do not acknowledge them or their power. Minimize everything they do. Then you can laugh, because now they're in rejection, and they throw a fit. The devil has asked me, "Do you know who I am?" And I minimize his words by saying, "You don't know who you are?!"

Demons cannot operate with someone like that because they're in rejection. Evil spirits will set the bar low, which makes it hard to obtain your goals. Familiar spirits drive you in rejection; if they can't push you, they'll pull you. You can prevent familiar spirits from influencing you by being led by the Lord, rather than being dragged by spirits, because sheep are meant to be led. When a familiar spirit is assigned to you, you disable it by ignoring it and minimizing its influence.

We will discuss walking in the Spirit's power and what God says about us. The Lord will show you some truths about deliverance. As you read these questions, pray in the Spirit, and the Lord will give you understanding.

PRAYER

Father, in the name of Jesus, thank You for our friends who are reading this book right now. Father, I ask that Your Holy Spirit saturate the words on these pages. Thank You, Father, for the power of God moving in our midst. Thank You, Father, for deliverance all over the world right now.

Thank You, Father, for the holy fire, the blood of Jesus, and the Holy Spirit. Thank You, Father. Hallelujah! In Jesus's name. Amen.

PART I

Heaven and Demons

What did you see in Heaven about demons and deliverance? What did you see about different levels of devils?

In Heaven, I saw that demons are like rebellious dogs that don't want to listen. They are watching how you react to see how much they can get away with before you recognize their schemes and stop them. Surprisingly, I saw that the demons are packed in here, and there wasn't just one demon but five behind every tree. I discovered it was better to chop down the tree and uncover what they were hiding behind.

Warrior Notes removes the tree behind which the demons hide, exposes them completely, and enforces

Jesus's work on the cross. Jesus made a show of them openly, triumphing over them through the cross, destroying the works of the devil.

As Christians, we should be enforcing the work that Jesus did and executing something already done. The demons don't want you to know this because when you stand up and push them, they will have to back off. There are many more demons than what people think, and their aim is to access people in high levels of leadership. There is a cycle in the world: Government becomes corrupt and begins to persecute Christians. The only way to prevent this cycle is to be a prayerful, repentant nation. When a nation is not remorseful, a remnant arises and separates itself. As they pray, revival and a move of God comes, which we are now in.

I discovered that at least one or two demons are assigned to almost every person. Their sole assignment was to prevent each person from reaching their destiny or realizing a book was written about them. The demon keeps people from the revelation that they are free and redeemed by Christ Jesus. Sadly, people live and die without knowing Christ because evil spirits deceive them.

One day, I was praying for people commenting on my YouTube channel as I acknowledged that I saw their response. Unfortunately, there are thousands of viewers daily on all the social media venues, so I cannot respond to each person. A person wanted to leave Hinduism and accept Jesus, but the evil spirits were preventing him by manifesting in terrible ways. He was harassed and threatened at night by some beings to prevent him from leaving Hinduism.

> I discovered that at least one or two demons are assigned to almost every person. Their sole assignment was to prevent each person from reaching their destiny

Halfway through the video as he watched, he asked, "Can you pray for me?" As I read his request, I began praying for him, and he said, "Never mind. Something just left me, and I'm free, and I'm going to accept Jesus Christ as my Savior." Freedom came to that man because the evil spirit that had been hindering and threatening him lost its hold on him, and he was released. The hindrance may have been that the man had no one to explain salvation to him. The devil prevents people from the knowledge and understanding of God's purpose for their lives.

I saw in Heaven that these demons want to keep people from prospering, being healthy, and walking into their destiny. What God has for us is the absolute truth. The system is set up so that if you are sick, you never get well. The cycle of debt causes you to never have enough money to get out of debt. Demons are strategically working to shut people down, yet people who dedicate themselves to the devil will prosper. If you give your life to the devil in different fields that I won't mention, you'll go to number one. These people will testify how they went to number one in their profession as soon as they did the ritual and drank blood.

The devil doesn't want you to be healthy or well, to prosper, or to have good relationships. He doesn't want you to get free and know you can finish your book written in Heaven and be a history maker (Psalms 139:16). The devil knows he's done if you find that out. Warrior Notes wants to equip people to know about the enemy's schemes. We're telling people that freedom is available to those who wish to dedicate their lives to the Lord, and they will live eternally in Heaven. While they're down here, they will rule and reign. Our Father desires to give us the kingdom; I saw this and so much more in Heaven.

The demonic realm has different levels and assigned territories. They fight and don't like each other. In addition, the smaller beings do exactly what they are told.

When I was on an airplane, I learned that certain points were definite boundaries for territorial spirits. I could feel something in the spirit and could not go past a certain point. While flying over different cities and states every hour, I kept track of departures and arrivals. When there was a change in that city's spirit, I began to feel specific ways. Certain groups and levels of devils, including territorial ones, are definitely over state lines. On the plane, the devils were with the people, and the people responded in different ways in different cities.

Let us pray.

PRAYER:

Father, I thank You that You want everyone free of the devil. You want everyone to be prosperous and in good health even as their souls prosper. I thank You, Father, that You desire everyone to be delivered right now. Everyone has some demonic influence against them because we're in a broken, fallen world. I drive out every devil and break every power of every spirit right now in the name of Jesus. The blood of Jesus is against you, satan. The name of Jesus is against you. Devil, I drive you out; I break your power.

Right now, deliverance has come to your house. Hallelujah. There's a whole move of God, a complete move of God. I see the blood of Jesus covering all the Christians right now on the doorposts of their heart.

I break death. I break the power of death over everyone in Jesus's name. I speak life to your body and peace to your mind. Yes to deliverance in Jesus's name. Praise God. Thank You, Father. I thank You that all over the world, people understand what Paul was talking about in Ephesians 6.

We thank You for information, wisdom, and knowledge on all levels. Lord, we are thankful that we have authority and power, not just us individually but corporately as a group of believers. We have dominion over all the enemy corporately in the name of Jesus. I thank You, Lord, that believers worldwide will rise and be a corporate body and find a local body that they can fellowship with, pray with, and come into agreement with, a fellowship that comes against these evil spirits in Jesus's name. Amen.

What did the Holy Spirit show you while reading/praying through this question:

____

____

____

____

What is the difference between the smaller demons and those that come out by prayer and fasting?

Many people don't understand the different hierarchies and types of demons; some are undefinable. Honestly, I can't go into some of the things I have seen because I don't even know what to call them. Jesus gave us authority over the earthbound spirits, those on *terra firma*, meaning the earth.[1] These are serpents and scorpions that crawl on the ground.

In the hierarchy of angels, two of the ranking angels are cherubim and seraphim. Another one that is mentioned a few times in the Bible is the *teraphim,*[2] which is a singular object, a disgraceful thing, and a false god, an idol. One of the patriarch's wives, Rachel, was found to have this idol in her baggage.

> *At the time they left, Laban was some distance away, shearing his sheep. Rachel stole her father's household idols and took them with her.*
>
> **—Genesis 31:19 NLT**

1 *Merriam-Webster Dictionary,* s.v. "terra firma (n.)," accessed September 14, 2023, https://www.merriam-webster.com/Dictionary/terra%20firma

2 "H8655 - tərāp̄ îm - *Strong's Hebrew Lexicon* (KJV)," Blue Letter Bible, accessed September 14, 2023, https://www.blueletterbible.org/lexicon/h8655/kjv/wlc/0-1/.

Verse 34 says, "But Rachel had taken the household idols and hidden them in her camel saddle, and now she was sitting on them." It goes on to say that she wouldn't get up.

In Ephesians 6:12, Paul talks about four levels of darkness we fight against: principalities, powers, rulers of the darkness, and spiritual hosts of wickedness. Some of these are walking on the earth. Some of what happened before the flood has not been spoken of and can go very deep into theology. Many things were going on in the Old Testament, in the days of the flood, that resulted in certain types of hybrid creatures. Greek mythology tells us that there were not only giants but creatures that were part human and part animal.

However, all this information opens up a hornet's nest. Everyone has an opinion about it. What we need to understand is that there are certain levels or degrees of devils. Some are tiny creatures, but others are upright on their feet and legs and look more human. Some types respond quickly to a Christian praying and executing justice while others do not respond very quickly. Bones from the hybrid race, the Neanderthal type of people, have been discovered. That's why some people claim that we came from these cavemen. However, these hybrid members of that race who lived before the flood were destroyed because they were wicked. In the flood, God destroyed humans and hybrid species of animals, keeping only certain animals. Noah inspected those; they were perfect and brought into the ark.

Some smaller devils are part of something similar, possibly more animal-like. A camera took a photograph at night, and we have pictures of a demon that looked like a little raccoon. It was agitated because we had to cast him out. Others may look like little monkeys. Over the years, I've seen different types of beings completely out of a horror film. When I was younger, I used to watch movies, and I saw those demons portrayed in the movies. Movie producers can portray those creatures because they do exist.

After kids play Dungeons and Dragons and similar games, I have seen them draw pictures of demons. Alarmingly, I've seen these actual creatures that were in movies or on posters.

When encountering a territorial type of entity, a high-level entity, Jesus recommended that we would need to fast and pray (Mark 9:29). The reason is that most people aren't where they need to be spiritually. People like Smith Wigglesworth would pray and fast and tell these things to leave. Maybe we need to pray and fast as well so that we can get to where we can deal with certain levels. Generals in the faith have walked in authority, and the demons listened to them. When you are set apart, pray and fast, and meditate on the Word of God, then those devils will go, but you don't want to deal with some of them alone.

If I'm hitting the hornet's nest, I might as well whack it off the tree. When you read, if you're being honest and look at the Word of God, the Bible gives us authority over serpents and scorpions and all the power of the enemy. God mentioned serpents and scorpions, which are earthbound and crawl on their bellies. Some scholars believe the serpent lost its legs. I'm telling you that lucifer was on his feet, *helel.*[3] The serpent, nâḥâš, used to be upright too; they were all upright.[4] God took the serpent and cursed him and put him on his belly.

You can do the math because that whole reptilian race was destroyed. I believe this was God's quick judgment on that hybrid experiment. These rulers in high places look otherworldly, and when they look at you, if you're not ready for it, they can look right through you and act like they're not afraid of you. I've encountered beings who were threatening and distraught with me; I did not engage with them but walked away, laughing at them. They were nine feet tall, had hoods on, and were trying to drag me down into the caverns of the damned, which is a hole that leads into hell. Of course, the Lord would not let that happen.

I have also seen high-level beings in the heavens that you would call UFOs and aliens. I'm going through

3 "H1966 - hêlēl – *Strong's Hebrew Lexicon* (KJV)," Blue Letter Bible, accessed February 2, 2024, https://www.blueletterbible.org/lexicon/h1966/kjv/wlc/0-1/.

4 "H5175 - nāḥāš – *Strong's Hebrew Lexicon* (KJV)," Blue Letter Bible, accessed February 2, 2024, https://www.blueletterbible.org/lexicon/h5175/kjv/wlc/0-1/.

this because Paul mentions these levels, but he doesn't use those words (*aliens* or *reptilian*). We don't know everything and have different definitions today for these manifestations happening in the world. If you want to come against these higher-level entities, you're going to need a church and body with a strong pastor united in a community. Many people need to be on the same page, fasting and praying to see the power of the higher-level ones broken. They come to kill, steal, and destroy. You've probably seen their work but didn't even realize it.

For the most part, you will deal with the smaller, little ones in your house and neighborhood. You only need to use the name of Jesus, speak the Word of God, and be very bold. These things will leave if you stomp your foot. If a Christian prays in tongues and speaks the Word of God, these little beings (I call them fuzzball devils) will need to leave. They know you don't need to say a word; all you need to do is stomp your foot. However, those in the air are higher beings who look like fallen angels, but they are part human. What bothers me the most is that I have seen these otherworldly beings before they appeared in movies and I recognized them.

As a Christian, Jesus gave us the power and authority to trample on serpents and scorpions, on terra firma, the earth, as I mentioned before. I have seen Christians who went after these higher-level territorial beings on their own, and they have been killed in car crashes or died of cancer. I'm not telling you what to do, but what I know is you need a strong local church, a strong local body with people that can agree with you. You can pray against them, preach the gospel, and speak and bring light into your neighborhood, community, and nation. It begins with you and goes to your family, and you will get rid of most demons.

When you encounter spirits walking like human beings (some would call them ghosts), you must be bold, aggressive, and rough with them. When they come against you, you need to say, "Well, I'm just going to pray in tongues for two hours instead of an hour, and I'm going to pass out tracts. I'm going to go out and witness. If you don't leave, I will do this every day." You must change everything around, making it worse for them.

There are different levels, but you don't need to get hung up focusing on that. You need to know their goal is to stop you and break your momentum. They begin with the tiny, irritating beings, and if you tune into the spirit, you can hear these little ones scream. When you begin to feel irritated and don't know why, it is because if you could hear in the spirit, you would hear shrill voices screaming at you. Be sure that if you're going after the ones over territories that you do as Jesus did and spend time in prayer and fasting. Jesus lived a fasted life; He was always praying and was always ready.

As you can see, there is much information regarding this question of hierarchy levels in the demonic world.

> There are different levels of demons, but you don't need to get hung up focusing on that. You need to know their goal is to stop you and break your momentum.

I would encourage you to study and look up all the words Paul uses. It would take too long for me to go through every Greek word. If you do that study, you'll probably be able to read between the lines and understand what I'm not telling you.

As I have said, when coming against the principalities and powers over cities, states, and nations, you need a strong group of people. Never attempt this alone. I would also encourage you to be prayed up and Spirit-filled. Put on the armor of God. Unfortunately, I've seen people who could not handle the backlash of those endeavors. Teachings of this type are profound and should not be treated lightly.

Prayer:

Father, I thank You so much. What we need here, Father, is for everyone to have discernment. I thank You, Lord God, that we have an understanding of Your Word. Paul said that there are different levels of devils, and I thank You, Lord, that we have the armor of God and the sword of the Spirit. Father, we are equipped and well able to defeat the enemy. We have authority over all four levels: the principalities, the powers, the rulers of this world's darkness, and the spiritual wickedness in high places. We have been given authority over them. Some we are to come against by prayer and fasting, and deliverance will come from the corporate side through the church. I thank You, Lord God, as we gather corporately, we come against all these in the name of Jesus right now, and we break the power from the most diminutive, little fuzzy devil to the highest level.

We pray for all believers. Strengthen them, Father, in the name of Jesus. Lord, I see all those housewives stomping their feet as the house is cleared of all those lying devils. I thank You, Lord, that anything that is harassing their children goes in the name of Jesus. If we must pray and fast to take out devils, that's what we'll do, Lord. We don't know everything. We don't understand all those levels that Paul talked about, but we are open to learning. Please instruct us in the name of Jesus. The blood of Jesus is against you, satan, and you're under our feet. Every devil is under our feet in Jesus's name. We break that power in Jesus's name. Amen.

What did the Holy Spirit show you while reading/praying through this question:

____

____

____

____

What did you see in Heaven about authority?

What I saw in Heaven about authority is a lengthy subject, and I will try to sum it up while maintaining the integrity of the question. However, I do not have the space here to do this justice. I saw the Spirit, which is the Word of God, and I noticed our authority with the Word of God and the Spirit. The Word of God is the sword of the Spirit; it's the Spirit and the Word. I saw that the sword was ours. One side of the sword cuts our enemy, and the other cuts us and separates the soul from the spirit (Hebrews 4:12). The Word of God, the Spirit of God, shows you what's God and what's you, your personality. Your character is your spirit, but you have a soul.

At times, you don't know what's you and what's God; this happens to all of us. The Word of God will come in by the Spirit and separate right down the middle and show you what is of you and what is of God; this can happen in a flash at the altar. Knowing what God is saying to you might take a couple of weeks, and sometimes it takes years to understand what's going on. I believe we will see an acceleration of understanding in the last days in which we live. When it comes to authority, we've been given this sword, which we're to use to separate soul and spirit. We're also supposed to use it as a weapon against our enemy.

You have great faith when you have discernment about authority. The centurion in Matthew 8:5-13 understood authority, but Jesus didn't say you have great authority. Jesus said, "You have great faith."

The centurion said, "Jesus, you don't have to come to my house. Just speak a word, and it'll be done. I have men under me, and I'm under men. I'm told what to do. Then I tell people what to do. Whatever you say, it'll be done." (Author's paraphrase Matthew 8:8-9.) According to Jesus, that was great faith.

That's what I saw about authority in Heaven and on earth. Every demon knows that what I just told you is the absolute truth. Every devil knows that if you do anything with this, they are finished and will lose their influence in your life.

Prayer:

Father, I thank You that we understand and have established our authority in the name of Jesus. We have great faith because we're under authority and do what we're commanded. Lord, You're our Commander. We love You, and we obey You and Your commandments. Yes, we have great faith. We understand You, Lord. I thank You that all the devils know that we're in charge, in the name of Jesus. We take full authority. Thank You in the name of Jesus, by the blood of Jesus.

Thank You, Father, for the name of Jesus. Lord, we declare over all our friends, partners, and listeners, in the name of Jesus, every demon out there that's bothering our friends, we command you to stop in Jesus's name. I thank

You have great faith when you have discernment about authority.

You, Father God, that we have faith and will have that authority that fills us up right now. We have our faith to walk into situations and stand in agreement with others that demons will leave.

We have that faith that says that mountains can be moved. We have faith in the authority that those we are praying for will be healed in the name of Jesus. We are standing in authority right now in the name of Jesus. When we are gathered, we have the authority.

We have the authority to know that mountains can be moved when we walk with Jesus and stand with Him. We have the faith and authority to understand that when God is on our side, nothing can stand against us. We pray for everyone right now. Father, we thank You for Your plan and destiny for each person. Lord, I pray for those that have given up and have had this brain fog, saying, "Man, I can't go on with God." They've been distracted and derailed.

Lord, we pray they would get back in alignment with You, that they would get back in the love of God. The love of God covers all sins. The love of God will call you back to where you need to be. Father, we ask that You touch us in the mighty name of Jesus.

Lord, may they feel Your love. I pray that You would move like never before and get them back on track in Jesus's name.

Every devil is running a thousand ways; there'll be an invasion of the presence of God in every home in Jesus's name. Father, I thank You for breaking every chain around the world in these precious people. Lord, I thank You that there is freedom where the Spirit of the Lord is. Freedom is being released all over the world. Lord, I thank You for the power of God.

I ask You for the presence of the Lord to just come into this place right now. We will go from failure to overflow. May you be filled with joy as the book of Acts says. There was great joy in the city as people were healed and set free. There's going to be great joy in our homes. I thank You for breaking every chain and that You are teaching Your people how to keep themselves unspotted from the world, resist the devil, and walk in purity.

I break every spirit that's been harassing God's people. We say, go in the name of Jesus. Lord, we thank You for the power and authority that is in Your name. I thank You, Lord. I feel the heaviness falling off people. Lord, I thank You for setting Your people free. As the title of this book is, so shall we be Forever Free. We declare this in Jesus's name.

Thank you, Father, that in our lives, there is no deception. You've given us the truth, and the truth has made us free. Now, because we are free, we can bring that freedom to our families, and they will all be able to know the love of God the way we do. Because the family is clear now, we can go to the world. We can take the world with your love, glory, and change, bringing Heaven to earth because You are the King and Lord of our world. We want You to rule and reign over us so we can see what Heaven is like here on earth. We thank You for it, in Jesus's name. Amen.

What did the Holy Spirit show you while reading/praying through this question:

____

____

____

____

Can demons influence you without you knowing it and how?

Yes, demons can influence you without your knowledge. The greatest deception is when you don't know you're deceived. They deceive you without your knowledge through disinformation. You take information as the truth, and it's not. You believe the information you receive, and you act on it. That is the most straightforward answer.

One example of this is the serpent's conversation with Eve. There, you will find your answer. Eve was being told that she was missing something that she already had. The serpent talked to her as if she were somehow left out. Then the serpent said, "Well, don't you know, if you eat this, you'll be like God?" Genesis 3:5 says that Adam and Eve were made in the image of God. Being made in God's image is close to looking like God.

If you don't know that something is wrong, but it actually is wrong, that is a problem. For example, if the speed limit is 25 mph but you think it's 45 mph, you will get a ticket. You didn't know, but it's still wrong. Another example would be a sign on the beach that says No Swimming. The sign is there because of the dangerous riptide. If you don't see the sign and swim there, you could drown. What you don't know can hurt you.

That's how the devils do it. They make you think you're missing out when you're not. Or they make you believe you have something you don't have. It's all about deception. Like the intelligence agencies, they all operate on gathering information. At the same time, they operate in disinformation. They hand out data and tell people it's secret and not to share it with anybody. It's false information because they know everyone will whisper it. It goes around as being a fact, and then it sends people off in the wrong direction, which was the whole idea. The enemy uses the same strategy: giving out disinformation.

Let me use this analogy. Kathi and I didn't have much money when we got married. We were happy to find a tiny house on a mountain for five hundred dollars a month. We were barely making it, but we were married and happy. A friend of Kathi's called her one day and told her that her name was in the paper associated with some unclaimed property and that this property would be turned over to the state if Kathi didn't contact them by the deadline. Kathi called the number, and by the end of the process, she had eleven thousand dollars, which was unexpected and came out of nowhere. The money belonged to Kathi the whole time; it was in

> You should always be reading the Word of God and investigating the truth, not just facts, because facts can change.

her name. It had already been held for her and given to her, but she didn't know it.

We are like that. We think, *How are we going to pay our bills*? You have an inheritance waiting for you because you are a child of God, yet you're always worried about paying your bills. This disinformation is the deception of the devil. That is how I see the devil; deceiving people without the individuals knowing it. He gets them to believe things that aren't true. That's why you should always be reading the Word of God and investigating the truth, not just facts, because facts can change.

Governments like to give information, and then they might say, "We're just kidding" when it doesn't work or when people don't believe the data. Science is discovery, observation. Science changes as scientists observe the facts. The absolute truth in Heaven may not be observable, but it's still true. Whatever God said, that's it. Eve didn't take what God said as the absolute truth. The serpent was negotiating with her and presenting twisted facts.

PRAYER:

Father, in the name of Jesus, I thank You so much. We break the spirit of deception. We pray, Lord, just like Paul did for the

Ephesians that we would have eyes to see and ears to hear. Father, we want to know the truth to which we've been called. We have set our sights on things above where Christ is seated at the right hand of God with full authority. I thank You, Father, that we will not be deceived. We'll know, Father, that as the clouds have rain, we are full of water as well. We are full of the truth. We pray in the Spirit. We walk in the Spirit. We see in the Spirit. We discern the truth of God's Word, do the works of Jesus, and drive out the devils in Jesus's name. We break deception in Jesus's name. Amen.

What did the Holy Spirit show you while reading/praying through this question:

How do we address demons and where should we send them?

You need to address demons roughly, be mean, and very strong about it. Think about this as though you were in law enforcement. You enforce the kingdom as an ambassador; therefore, you use authority. You're firm and you don't argue with them. You continue to give the command. Don't back off, and don't reason with them.

In one incident, Jesus sent demons into a herd of pigs. However, the demons asked for permission to go there first. This is not a model for us to follow. Other than that, I'm not aware of any place in the Bible where anyone sent demons to a specific place. Jesus just cast them out. The demons would ask Him not to send them to the pit or torment them before their time. They requested not to be sent to the pit, which indicates He could have sent them there. They requested not to be sent out of the area. He didn't torment them before their time or send them out of the area. It's not clear in the Bible where they were sent. We don't send them anywhere.

Jesus said devils go to arid places when you cast them out (Matthew 12:43). That would seem the safest place to send them from what I can tell.

We must be honest and ask questions. Why didn't Jesus send them to the pit? Why didn't He send them out of the area? Why did He pick on the pigs? They were unclean animals. There are no easy answers except that we cast them out, and in this instance, they went into arid places. If you cast them out, they're returning to see if they can gain entrance again. We focus on sealing the entry point so the people are ready for the demons when they want to try to gain entrance again.

Paul said that after we've done everything to stand, stand against the enemy (Ephesians 6:13). In other words, after you take a stand against the devil, then plant your feet. Stay there and don't move. Stand. That's the biblical way to do it. All the other methods are like a friendly discussion, but we don't know what we can and cannot do except drive them out. I'm big on discipleship and educating people so the devil can't return.

PRAYER:

Father, in the name of Jesus, I thank You for addressing the demons boldly because You've given us authority and power over all the enemies, and nothing by any means shall harm us. We firmly come against the enemy, in Jesus's name. Father, we know that when we send the demons out, they go into arid places and suffer, and we're happy for that. We thank You, Lord, that the job we've been instructed to do is to fortify the person so that the demons cannot return to fill them up. We teach them the Word of God. Thank You, Father. We receive these things in the name of Jesus. Hallelujah. Amen.

After you take a stand against the devil, then plant your feet. Stay there and don't move.

What did the Holy Spirit show you while reading/praying through this question:

____

____

____

____

> If someone cannot overcome a demonic attack, how can we stand with them and break it?

The Bible refers to a church, a bride, or a body without spots or wrinkles, being united, mature, and full of faith. Jesus asked, "When the Son of Man comes, will he find faith on the earth?" (Luke 18:8). You can conclude that the body is fully equipped, weaned off milk, mature, and without spot or wrinkle. Finally, they love each other. Jesus said you'd know them by their love, and the world will see that so that deliverance will result.

You overcome every single time by showing the love of God. You may not see instantaneous results. At times, it took a couple of years, but without exception, every time I have loved someone, and they were manifesting devils, sometimes it only took days for that person to turn around. Sometimes it takes two or three years, but eventually, love causes that devil to lose its grip.

I experienced this every week at work. By the end of any particular work week, the love of God had made His presence known, and those demons had to leave. I often witnessed the devil clinging to a person, causing them to manifest. Some people were super hard to work with, but I loved them. As the days went by, I continually prayed for those individuals.

Eventually, my determination to love them made the devil slippery like he had oil on him. The devil was losing his grip as God's love was poured out. Toward the end, the devil was barely hanging on to the ankles. The love of God enabled the person to get saved, and they would break down and cry. That devil would be wholly removed because love conquers all. That's what 1 Corinthians 13 is all about: love. The devils cannot operate in love. Love paralyzes demons. That's how we stand against a demonic attack that seems unbreakable.

PRAYER:

Father, I thank You that love conquers all. I thank You, Lord. We could be spiritual giants and move mountains, but we're nothing if we don't have love. I thank You, Father, for showing us how to break the demonic, those complex cases, through our love. We need to love people and stay with them.

When we love on them, the devil loses his grip. We pray that You would baptize them with Your love, Father. I thank You that the devils are losing their grip and

Love paralyzes demons.

that the body of Christ, the glorious church, is rising to take its rightful place in these last days. They're going to know us by our love. I thank You for it. In the name of Jesus. Amen.

What did the Holy Spirit show you while reading/praying through this question:

____

____

____

____

What do you do when a spirit doesn't leave you?

People think the devil is hard of hearing, so they talk louder; therefore, you tend to take "no" for an answer. I refuse to take "no" for an answer. I also listen to the Spirit at the same time. When the Lord wants to give me a word of knowledge regarding why a demon is present, I listen. I have found that the devil has a legal reason to be there. The devil believes he has ownership of the person.

You'd be surprised at how demons can be attached to some gifts in your house. We don't want to be superstitious, but if a witch or an evil spirit prayed over an object, these items must be removed or, at the very least, prayed over. In the shops in these countries where these items are sold, they put voodoo curses on certain objects. You might think everything's fine, but if you allow that item in your house, you might need to teach that devil a lesson. After all, the evil spirit might follow the given item because it's cursed. You don't want these objects in your house. If you do some research, you will easily find a list of things that you should not have in your home.

In some places in the Bible, certain types of creatures or animals were considered part of a curse. God had judged them in the desert. Job 30:29 talks about where only the jackal and the owl dwell, and there was mention of a curse. You might think certain animals are cute, but they represent evil. In other words, do not bring an object set apart as cursed into your house, an item that symbolizes some sort of idol from an evil religion or the occult.

There have been times when the Lord has told me to set an object apart as holy (sanctify it through prayer), and I have never had a problem with it. You may have something in your house that looks demonic, and it may affect a weaker brother or sister. What if they see a skull or some other item in your house? It's probably a bad idea to have something like that in your home anyway.

Even if you could pray away all the devils or whatever you feel has followed the item, it still represents something cursed or profane. I would not have a skull or items that represent death in my house. I would not have certain objects representing evil that people with a weaker faith cannot understand.

As Paul said, if a person asks if this meat was sacrificed to idols, there's nothing wrong with that. It was set apart with prayer and blessing if you bless it. But if they're weak in their faith, don't serve that meat to them. You tell them it has been used as a sacrifice, and you honor their conviction and give them meat that wasn't used as a sacrifice.

In Corinth, the meat used for sacrifices had been cut up and offered to the idols. They set it on a plate and offered it to these gods. After the sacrificial offering, the meat was cheaper to buy. Since it was less expensive, some families bought it instead. When the Christian congregation began to grow in Corinth, they said you couldn't eat it because it was presented to an idol. But Paul clearly states that if it was set apart and a Christian blessed the meat, there was nothing wrong with eating it. Paul also said to honor and respect people with weaker faith.

In the same way, some people might have a problem with an item in your home because that's where their faith is set. You must not have certain objects in your house: Ouija boards and similar items, such as tarot cards or those that relate to astrology or witchcraft. Those are genuine tools used by the satanic realm for inquiring into the spiritual realm and are all definitely forbidden in the Bible.

If a spirit doesn't want to leave, you must find out why. A Christian must determine what authority the evil spirit thinks they have or perhaps does have. If a devil speaks up, I will ask that devil what gives them the right to be there. I ask, "How did you enter?" After they tell me, I command them to shut up. Then I bring the person back, and I talk to them. I say, "Do you know you have this devil?" They say yes. Then I tell the person that the devil said they want to keep the spirit, and I ask them if that is true. If the person says, "Yes, I want to keep the evil spirit," they must repent.

If a spirit doesn't want to leave, you must find out why.

Once, a person told me how the devil was allowed to enter. It confirmed what the devil said, and that the person didn't want to give up that sin that had allowed the devil to reside in that person. I said, "Then you and that devil are going to hell unless you repent." He didn't repent and went to jail that night. Unfortunately, that devil was still talking through him as they took him away.

Devils should leave when you tell them to go. If they don't, you need to find out why. If a person is not born again, they need to be born again before you cast the devil out. A devil should not be manifesting if a person is a born-again believer. In this case, you must find out what legal right that devil has that enabled them to do what they're doing.

Most of the time, with a Christian, these matters are quickly taken care of because they are born-again with the Spirit inside them. God is in there, and these demons that bother them would be in their soul realm: mind, will, and emotions. You can remove them, but the person must cooperate. However, if the devils are not leaving, if they're mouthing off, if the problem is chronic and they keep coming back, or if nothing is happening, then you must have a sit-down with them. Tell them, "Listen, a man is going to reap what they sow. You've sown something because you're reaping this, and it's mocking God, but God will not be mocked. It's you—it's not God." You must be firm with people because if you are not, you won't be able to deal with that devil.

I've been through this many times, and people want to be free and stay free; therefore, you can't give the enemy access. Remember that if the devil has entered due to a traumatic event, they must be healed. They need to go through counseling. They need to work through those emotions and process them so that permanent deliverance can occur. If I'm dealing with the devil, I always get to the bottom of the problem. There's always some final result. Even if the devil stays in a person, I know why. I do not let anyone go until the person decides what they will do.

All the demonic on the earth happens because men and women do not understand who they are. We are above familiar spirits; therefore, we don't need their assistance. People think they need the aid of these familiar spirits, but we don't because we're at a higher level. When we're redeemed, we get the first inclination of who we are in Christ, and the devils must leave. The battle is now in your mind, will, and emotions, and that is because it moves out from your spirit, which God occupies. I want to make this point clear: There is a resolution as far as evil spirits go.

At times, some people have something physically wrong with them. Biologically, they have something wrong in their brain. They have certain clinical problems as well. Sometimes, Jesus didn't cast the devil out but just prayed for their healing. There is a difference between healing and a miracle. Healing is when God takes what you have and does something with it. But a miracle is when God must form something that's not there, like an arm, and that is a miracle, not a healing. Sometimes Jesus needed to perform a miracle because the person had a defect, even something missing, and God had to restore that person to wholeness. Not everything is a devil because part of our troubles are due to living in a fallen world. Rest assured, we know that devils must leave.

Many people are struggling and in need of answers, but spiritual fights go on for years because we're dealing with people's wills. Kathi and I have been in many spiritual battles where we would not have seen the victories if we had given an inch. We were sent to help churches by fighting battles. I can look back and say that we would not have had the same result if we had given up. However, we didn't give an inch but became more aggressive. It looked like the devils wouldn't leave. Eventually, their power broke.

Once, we moved to another city and bought a house just because God said to help this pastor and support this church. It took two or three years of praying, fasting, and breaking the devil's power. Then one week, the pastor announced that we would have twenty-four-hour prayer, and he asked people to fill the slots during the day. No one signed up from midnight to three, so Kathi and I said we'd take it. Everyone had come to the church to take their appointed time slot. We came in at midnight, praying in the spirit until three, but we liked it so much we stayed all night until six.

Within two weeks, while people prayed in the church, the manifest glory of God fell. As they walked toward me, the pastor and his assistant fell in the Spirit and had to crawl to me. Then I fell. This also happened with the pastor's kids; they were on the floor near the altar. That same Holy Spirit power carried over to the Sunday service when everyone showed up for choir and band practice. The service was to begin at 10:00 a.m.; however, the Holy Spirit showed up at band practice with the choir singing. There was a packed house at 8:00 a.m., and the congregation worshipped for two hours. The pastor got up but had difficulty standing and could hardly preach because the Holy Spirit was so powerful. The entire congregation felt the impact of the Holy Spirit's move. Every service for nearly a year ended with people on the floor, including ushers, and you just got up when you could and showed yourself out.

It all began when we beat back the enemy and refused to let the devil tell us "no." Through our obedience to move to this city, God used us as we fasted and prayed with the pastor, staff, board members, and family members. Demonic influences broke, and we never felt the devil in those services. Everyone wanted to come.

We are in the same season right now. When a devil won't leave, we refuse to take that as the final answer in the name of Jesus.

PRAYER:

I break the enemy's power right now in all the churches on earth, Father. I pray there'll be a great and mighty move of Your Spirit and the lost would come in and the sick would be healed. Father, I pray that the demons would be driven out and the gospel would be preached. Jubilee would be announced, and that the people would be debt-free in the name of Jesus. Father, I thank You for everything. We come against all stubborn devils. We break their power right now in the name of Jesus, all those hard places that people have experienced. We drive you out, satan. In Jesus's name. Hallelujah.

What did the Holy Spirit show you while reading/praying through this question:

____

____

____

____

How do demons and sickness work together?

Sometimes Jesus cast out a devil when people were sick, and sometimes He just prayed for the person, and they were made well. The natural part of sickness is when illness and disease occur in people's bodies. The origin is because of sin; the root is because of a fallen, broken world. News flash: We'll all die in our physical bodies unless the rapture occurs. If the Lord comes back and grabs you, takes you to Heaven, and doesn't return you, you're an exception.

Sickness is part of the fall, so sickness and disease are part of the fallen world that we live in. However, because of the covenant, certain truths overrode what was happening in the environment. For instance, Paul said that the law of sin and death was still at work, but he said that the power of the law of the spirit of life would break the power of the law of sin and death. In other words, a more significant law was at work.

If you want to fly, you get in an airplane, taxi onto the runway, and sit there. You're sitting in an airplane but won't go anywhere because you can't overcome gravity. However, increasing your speed creates the thrust and the lift from the wings; those two things can overcome gravity if everything goes well. You make that forward or upward motion and reverse the effects of gravity that have been created.

> *There is therefore now no condemnation for those who are in Christ Jesus. For the law of the Spirit of life has set you free in Christ Jesus from the law of sin and death. For God has done what the law, weakened by the flesh, could not do. By sending his own Son in the likeness of sinful flesh and for sin, he condemned sin in the flesh.*
>
> —**Romans 8:1–3 ESV**

When a law presented is through the Spirit, it usurps authority over sin and death. He explains that you must take the misdeeds and come against the body's transgressions with the Spirit. The Spirit puts to death the misdeeds of the body. Paul says he was trapped in certain sins. He's saying you can tap into something more significant, and you will stop doing those sins, according to Romans 7. Then in Romans 8, Paul says the Spirit of life will put to death the misdeeds of the body, usurping authority over sin and death. Within the covenant, there is a way to receive healing, deliverance, and financial and spiritual help.

You might be dealing with a sickness. Perhaps you are in the wrong environment, not eating right, or have something handed down to you genetically in your DNA. It is crucial to understand that because of the fall, the devil is behind sickness and disease. For example, you may have symptoms where the uric acid is not filtered out of your body, creating problems with your kidneys. Maybe you only have one functioning kidney. Biological problems and birth defects happen because of the fall.

We understand that the fallen world is a curse from satan, the god of this world. When we focus on the covenant, we must discern whether symptoms are biological or a demon is causing them. I have had physical evidence that when the devil left, the manifestation left. However, at other times, people were healed, and it wasn't the devil. Jesus did both: He prayed for the sick or cast out the devil. The bottom line is that everything comes from the fallen and broken world. Yet, it doesn't hurt to address the devil anyway. If I can't discern what the root of the problem is, I come against the enemy in Jesus's name and pray for the person to be healed.

When we focus on the covenant, we must discern whether symptoms are biological or a demon is causing them.

I have mostly prayed for people to be healed and for the devil to leave them, but I didn't address the devil. I only prayed for their healing. Unless you have the discerning of spirits, which is a gift of the Holy Spirit so that you can tell what it is, you will pray for their healing. I have had that gift operating in my life, and people asked me, "Is this a devil or just a biological issue?"

I said, "Well, there's no devil anywhere near you. You must go to a doctor and let them diagnose you. Then we can pray for your healing. After we pray, return to the doctor and let him tell you his opinion." That happened to us. We were on medication, and I said, "Well, I won't have that long." As we speak, I'm working my way out of that right now.

We went back to the doctor, who said, "It's gone. But you had it." He showed me the tests for kidney failure and liver problems. I let the doctor give me a clean bill of health, and I would recommend you do the same.

How do you discern if it's a devil or a sickness? Realize the devil is probably behind it. He's probably within the city block of it. I always blame him anyway. As far as getting your healing, God heals. This must be addressed if an evil spirit is present, making that manifestation happen.

PRAYER:

I thank You, Lord, that if anyone is experiencing symptoms in their body, anything that they're going through with their body, we pray for their healing right now in the name of Jesus. You're the healer. We are just going to believe for a miracle, Lord God. We know You are the healer, and we're praying and agreeing with the body of Christ. Everyone out there, receive your healing right now in the name of Jesus. If a devil is anywhere near your body, we break that power in Jesus's name and drive out the devil. Bye-bye. Thank you, Father. Thank You, Lord, for healing us. Thank You, Jesus, for Your suffering so that we could receive healing, according to Isaiah 53, in the name of Jesus. Amen.

What did the Holy Spirit show you while reading/praying through this question:

PART II

Deliverance

How do we pray for deliverance for a loved one who is not living for God?

Now, this is a difficult situation because of people's free will and because of authority. The one thing that the devil does understand is authority. We must learn to walk in authority. So if you understand this, build up your faith, and learn to walk in these truths, you can then exercise your authority.

However, when taking authority over another person, there's a better way to gain some leverage on the devil instead of just trying to cast him out of someone who might not even want the demon out. In this instance, we are talking about praying for deliverance for a loved one who is not living for God. I will pray this prayer in Ephesians 1:17–23 over them so they can see and know where they're at and what God has for them.

> *Asking God, the glorious Father of our Lord Jesus Christ, to give you spiritual wisdom and insight so that you might grow in your knowledge of God. I pray that your hearts will be flooded with light so that you can understand the confident hope he has given to those called—his holy people who are his rich and glorious inheritance. I also pray that you will understand the incredible greatness of God's power for us who believe. This is the same mighty power that raised Christ from the dead and seated him in the place of honor at God's right hand in the heavenly realms. Now he is far above any ruler or authority or power or leader or anything else—not only in this world but also in the world to come. God has put all things under the authority of Christ and has made him head over all things for the benefit of the church. And the church is his body; it is made full and complete by Christ, who fills all things everywhere with himself.*
>
> **—Ephesians 1:17–23 NLT**

In the case of an unsaved loved one, salvation must become part of the equation. If a person is not saved, they need to be born again. A person who is not saved has no authority over the devil. You can beat the devil up and punch them and get even with them, but they are coming back because that person was not cooperating with God. And they will not cooperate if you try to deliver them unless they are willing. They need to get on the same side of Christ, so you must win them over in the soul. That's what Solomon said here: "The fruit of the righteous is a tree of life, and whoever captures souls is wise" (Proverbs 11:30 ESV).

The word *soul* does not mean "spirit," so we are not winning spirits but souls. In the Old Testament, they didn't have the born-again experience. Solomon said you must win somebody over in their mind, will, and emotions. He said you are wise if you do that because that person will come into agreement with you and no longer work against you.

Witches come to almost every one of our services. They will come up and repent because they've come to try to damage the service, and their witchcraft doesn't work. They give their life to Christ. I ask them right away, "Are you done with the devil? Are you finished with him? Are you going to sever your relationship with the devil?" When they say yes, they are on the same page. Now they've decided to come to the Lord, and I lead them in the salvation prayer. As soon as we're done with

You must win somebody over in their mind, will, and emotions.

the salvation prayer, the devils begin to leave. I don't even have to touch that person. The person doesn't want them anymore, so the devils come out because they know they must leave.

Since we are speaking about an individual who is not a Christian, you need to pray that the eyes of their heart would be enlightened to know the hope to which they have been called. Then ask the Lord to send some sort of ambassador in their path, other than you, to talk to them about Jesus. I pray harvesters into the field and that someone not attached to me is sent to them. Once you convince them to side with you, permanent deliverance will happen because the playing field is even. I don't want the devil to come back. The devils return if a person does not entirely understand what's happening. However, most new Christians don't know or understand what's happening.

The point here is about access. Do you give that devil access? If people are not being taught these principles, the demon spirit is coming back, not just the one that was cast out but seven more with him, according to Jesus (Matthew 12:43–45). It is paramount to educate people regarding deliverance and that we get to the source or root of the problem, because if we do not, the devils either don't leave or return.

That person must come into agreement with God and decide to turn back and serve the Lord. They agree they're not going to date the devil during the week and serve God on weekends at church. Then you pray over them and break the power of the devil, but ensure they know the devil will try to come back. The demon will present that point of entry or temptation to entice that person to return to bondage. When people aren't living for God, are they strong enough to make the right decision? We must uncover the root of why the devil has access to them. No one made them do this, but they made their own decision and choice. They went through a process and chose to allow this demon to gain entrance and obtain residence to influence them.

You must pray for your loved one to walk with God. Pray that the Spirit of God opens their eyes, that they have an amazing revelation of God's love. Once they know God's love, that will lead them to repentance. Then you can get them to agree with you about any access the demons have. This access is different for everyone. Certain devils are assigned to people. This is generational.

These demons are more persistent and disciplined than people and have nothing to lose. They can't win, and they can't be redeemed. They will just go all out against a person. So, if you have a loved one, you must get their relationship right with God first, whether it's salvation or coming back to God through repentance. Then ask them some questions. Why are these devils allowed to enter? Find out what the access point is. Jesus questioned them and asked, "What happened to your child?

What does this devil do?" Then He determined what type of spirit it was and cast it out.

Prayer:

Father, I want to pray for all those who have loved ones they are praying for who need deliverance. Father, we understand that it's all about authority and all about the healing of a person's soul. Father, we ask that You give them wisdom and the ability to discern to pray according to the relationship part of this person. We pray, Father, for all the loved ones, that the eyes of their hearts would be open and that they would know the hope to which they've been called. We pray, Father, that they would know the glorious inheritance in the saints and see the indwelling power that rose Jesus from the dead.

I thank You, Father, that if these loved ones are not saved, You will lead an ambassador to them so that they may come to know the need for their salvation and that they can be saved and delivered through prayer. We pray that they will see deliverance and salvation. Lord, if they are away from God, we ask that they will come back. If they need saving, we ask that they will receive it.

Father, we thank You for the movement of Your Spirit right now. Father, we pray that the loved ones will make a move right now in the name of Jesus. The blood of Jesus is against you, satan. We thank You, Father, that all those loved ones are coming in. We believe they will agree with the Word of God. We agree with them, Lord, that deliverance will be complete and the healing will come. Whatever it is that's allowing that devil to have access to them, we break that in Jesus's name. We are thankful that the hindrance will be revealed, and that the resolution of Jesus Christ will manifest. We acknowledge that the loved ones are coming in for fullness of deliverance and salvation in Jesus's name. Amen.

What did the Holy Spirit show you while reading/praying through this question:

____

____

____

____

How should we approach deliverance with children?

As parents, you have authority over your children, but not all children will have a level of understanding. If you're a teacher, then you have authority over your students. I have authority over any Warrior Notes student *if* they recognize and honor that authority. Then I can speak over them and take authority because they're under me.

This relationship and authority between teachers and students is similar to when the disciples submitted to Jesus. He could exercise authority, and miracles would happen for the disciples. However, He couldn't perform miracles for other people outside that influence, like in His hometown. His relatives weren't even healed.

You have authority over your children if they are under your care. Pray over them and speak the Word of God over them. Anoint them with oil, read Bible stories, or play Christian music before bed. According to some reports, parents have played music in their children's rooms all night, and they have been delivered from demons. When the parents played godly music and the Word of God over their children, their kids had dreams and visions. I recommend this. As you saturate their minds with prayer, worship music, and the Bible during the night, this protects your child. Children can comprehend spiritual matters if you teach them at a young age to take authority over the devil. They are submitted to your care; you can pray and intercede for them and keep the devil away.

I find myself talking about controversial subjects in the Bible all the time, such as prosperity, speaking in tongues, the devil, deliverance, oppression, depression, and possession. I have seen friendly pet animals turn and become influenced by evil spirits. I have also seen kids who did not know what was happening, but they acted out in manifestations when they've growled like an animal. I've had kids say in a deep voice, "I don't like you." And I'm thinking, *"I don't like you either."*

When a devil is influencing a child, I don't think it is fair that a devil should touch them. I don't understand why this happens. I have seen these manifestations with a child; however, I don't want to pretend this problem is not happening by not addressing it. I want the child to be free. I have told the demon, "You come out of him in the name of Jesus," and they have left. I then have the children say that Jesus is Lord, and I pray with them. Children are attacked at night with bad dreams from devils, and I have seen video footage where objects are moving in the children's rooms.

The bottom line is we need to care, protect, and cover our children with the blood of Jesus.

The bottom line is we need to care, protect, and cover our children with the blood of Jesus. Whether or not you believe demons exist or children can be tormented, there is a satanic problem in this world. A person will deny a devil exists, yet the demon is standing right behind them. My problem with the church is their denial that these demons exist.

This is a complicated subject, and some prefer to pretend these things do not happen. We can tell when the devil is operating. Some might say the Christian is demon possessed. But the exact answer to this doesn't really matter. The fact is, if a devil is present in a person, whether they are a Christian or not, it must be cast out. This is the practical application. Let's stop arguing about these matters and truly help set people free.

Imagine the frustration when a parent is facing these demonic influences in their child and they come for help. What if you counsel them that you don't believe in demons and pretend it isn't happening?

After that session, the parent goes to their car and thinks, *What do we do next?* They are still left with a problem with the child. The denial of demons and their power has been the problem with Christianity and the body of Christ. But this has gotten worse because we've ignored the facts and what's happening, thinking it will improve. The next four years will be better, yet it doesn't get better because we keep deferring it, denying what is happening around us in society. What happens if we lay hands on these small children as Jesus did? Here is one example.

> *He asks the boy's father, "How long has this been going on?"*
>
> *"Ever since he was a little boy. Many times it pitches him into fire or the river to do away with him. If you can do anything, do it. Have a heart and help us!"*
>
> *Jesus said, "If? There are no 'ifs' among believers. Anything can happen."*
>
> *No sooner were the words out of his mouth than the father cried, "Then I believe. Help me with my doubts!"*
>
> *Seeing that the crowd was forming fast, Jesus gave the vile spirit its marching orders: "Dumb and deaf spirit, I command you: Out of him, and stay out!" Screaming, and with much thrashing about, it left. The boy was pale as a corpse, so people started saying, "He's dead." But Jesus, taking his hand, raised him. The boy stood up.*
>
> **—Mark 9:21–26 MSG**

Jesus didn't argue with them about possession, oppression, and depression; He got rid of the spirit and cast it out. Whether the person is young or old, we may use different techniques, but we acknowledge and deal with demons by casting them out. When Jesus got close to people, the demons began to manifest, and He didn't even say anything.

You don't need to deal with devils by looking for them, because you'll run into them everywhere you go. Walking right with God is the key—you're sent. When you go to the grocery store to buy food, look at it as being on a mission because the Lord is going with you. Every time you go to church, pray about someone you can bless. When you stay in the Word and prayer, God will use you and give you a word for somebody.

Kathi and I would take money that we set aside and pray. "Lord, who do you want us to give this to today?" I intentionally put money in my pocket and said to myself, *I'm not coming home with this money, and this money is not mine anymore.* I asked for direction on where we were to give it. This money was over and above our offering.

You deal with the devil the same way. When you walk up to a person, you don't need to ask if any devils are in there. No, you don't need to do that. Jesus never did that; He dealt with people as they came. He asked some basic questions, such as "How often has this happened?" Then He asked different questions, and then He addressed the devil and cast it out. He then got them something to eat, and that was it. That's how I deal with each situation as it comes up. I train the students to get before the Spirit and be sent and go.

As Christian parents, take authority over the devils and do not allow them in your house. Pray and anoint your child to be set apart for God under your authority.

PRAYER:

Lord, I plead the blood over children right now. I speak to the parents that if you've been opening the door to evil, if you've been arguing, if you've been allowing unclean items in your home, you need to repent. I pray that they will begin to close the doors in their homes and be the coverings that God has created them to be. Every devil, every demon coming against their dreams and trying to overwhelm or distract them, we plead the blood right now, in Jesus's name. We declare that these kids will be free to flow in the Holy Ghost, walk in their callings, use their gifts, and live for Jesus in His name. Every assignment against their innocence is broken right now. We declare that right now in the name of Jesus.

We thank You, Father, that every home out there will be filled and flooded with the power and presence of Jesus. Father, I pray right now, if any child needs deliverance, the parents will take the authority they've been given in the name of Jesus. I pray that the parents would lay hands on their children and anoint them with oil. The children will be set apart for Your plan and purpose as it is written in Heaven in the name of Jesus. We break all the behavior problems in the name of Jesus right now. I drive out rebellion in Jesus's name. I take authority, and I thank You, Lord. You're giving the parents and teachers the boldness to take power over those devils. You must leave the children alone, satan, in Jesus's name.

Father, I thank You so much. In the name of Jesus, we thank You, Lord, that You give us wisdom. We will even be told the words to say. We will say yes when we need to. We won't worry about what to say because like Jesus said, You will give us the right words when it's time. I thank You, Lord, that You will take control in every situation. We've been commanded—not requested but commanded—to go forth, preach the gospel, cast out devils, heal the sick, raise the dead, and preach jubilee that debts have been canceled.

I thank You, Father, that in the name of Jesus, if devils get in the way, they will be kicked out. That's just the way it's going to be. In Jesus's name. Amen.

What did the Holy Spirit show you while reading/praying through this question:

____

____

____

____

How do we deal with generational spirits?

Regarding generational spirits, the bottom line is that some people disagree. I'm not here to get people to change their minds—God does that. We are commanded to lay hands on the sick—that's what you do. You lay hands on them, and God heals them. You cast out the devils. You tell them to leave, and they go because of the authority of Jesus, not because you're anything apart from Jesus. You can deal with generational spirits in the same way. We have understanding and knowledge, and we can share that, but we can't make somebody believe something. They must mix the Word with faith in their relationship with God. Some people don't agree with the whole idea of generational spirits; however, I know this concept is true.

I was shown that spirits are assigned to bloodlines. However, I was also shown that they are beaten and whipped if they do not do what they're told. They are to enforce the curse to generations. The only time they stop is when someone who discerns what's going on comes in, takes authority over it and destroys it. The bottom line is this: You're the one that's assigned to break generational curses in your own family. You're the one; it's not the next generation. It wasn't your grandma because if she's passed on, it's up to you now. Every person must take a stand against generational curses and generational spirits.

Now, they are disembodied from the flood and are on earth. They don't want to leave their area because they know they will be tormented, but it's not time yet. They know the people walking with God because they can see the people of God, the sons of God, glow. They can see the angels coming back and forth and visiting you. These spirits are in the location they were before the flood.

Many, many people were on the earth. If you do the research, millions of people were on the earth at the time of the flood. If you take all the genealogies, people lived to be nine hundred years old. You can have a lot of kids in nine hundred years. This has expanded, and these spirits are assigned to families because they will not be redeemed. They will not get any relief through good behavior; there's no redemption. They are going to wreak havoc.

They are assigned to their area, and you can sense the change from region to region. Sometimes it's better to have someone from another area come in and lambaste the devil for you. It works because those devils ask, "Who is this?" They can't perform their junk on that person because they're not from that area. Many issues are entrenched because the demons reside in these locations. Some people refuse to live where I live because of the demons in my region. The devil will beat the living daylights out of you. God trusts me, so I am free and can live where I do without being bothered. God entrusts all of us to be in the region we live in because we can handle it; we're not going anywhere. You must see that the devil is going somewhere, but you are not.

These curses and generational spirits follow the bloodlines but are also assigned to a specific location. After two or three years, I gained the momentum to break their influence over me when I left the place where I grew up. When I returned, I could feel the evil presence and that the same spirits were there, but they weren't going with me when I left.

Yet the familiarity of my family members and of being back in that same place created that spiritual environment of bondage. After a while, I got deliverance so that when I returned, the devil had a fit. I began talking, and all my brothers and sisters received salvation. My parents got saved, and then the demons had an even bigger fit.

Finally, I got to the place where I was completely free of any demonic spirit I had grown up around. People began to tell me, "You need to move back and live here."

I said, "What did you just say?" I'm a grown man, and the demonic spirit was trying to influence me to move back.

People told me, "I want you to quit your job." People told me that if we were to have a relationship, I would leave my job because they wanted me to move there. They would say, "I don't care if you deliver pizzas. You're going to live here." I was thinking, *Really? What did you say?* I recognized that as a spirit, a territorial spirit.

Because of what I've encountered, I will tell you the truth to help you understand the way I teach and why you need to make deliverance permanent. These evil spirits want to follow the generation, but you're the one that can break the curse. My entire family has diabetes. A time came when I chose to break that curse over my life, so I received healing in my body. I said, "I will never have diabetes because I forbid that right now in the name of Jesus." I changed my diet and never ate sugar at all.

Occasionally, I have a piece of candy, but I choose not to eat sugar.

Everyone's waiting to see if I'm going to get diabetes, but I have had no hint of it, and I'm sixty years old now. I saw what was happening in my family and chose to stop the cycle of diabetes. Then I saw other illnesses or diseases in my friends where everyone in the family started encountering these problems. I recognized these as generational spirits, and they will even go into your pets.

One of my friends taught at the same university I taught at, and he invited me to go to Pakistan with him. He said, "There are a lot of terrorists and people who plant bombs there. But you can preach to huge crowds, five hundred thousand people."

I said I would pray about it. But I didn't go. He went into houses full of people hungry for generational curses to be broken. As he walked into one place, there were between thirty and sixty cats, and in unison, they began growling at him because the spirits had entered the cats. To deal with generational spirits, you must shut them down yourself.

In Romans 7:15, Paul said, "For what I am doing, I do not understand. For what I will to do, that I do not practice, but what I hate, that I do." I find myself not doing things I want to do. If you find yourself in that situation of Romans 7, according to Paul, you need to graduate to Romans 8. That is your place to live.

The generational curses and evil problems in your life all concern the flesh. Don't spiritualize it past that point. The devil keeps bothering you because you are the sole authority. You must say no to ungodliness and worldly possessions and live an upright life in Christ Jesus. It would be best if you recognize what Paul wrote as these are manifestations of the flesh and considered witchcraft (Galatians 5:20).

However, that's your assignment, just like David's assignment was to take out Goliath. There is no other war you must fight but familiar spirits and generational curses; it's your turn, so begin swinging. If you can't stop doing something you want to do, then a spirit is assigned to you. You can check it out and investigate it further by talking to a grandparent, a parent, a sibling, or a family member. It's amazing how these problems get turned over to the next generation, yet the previous generations don't speak of them. Very rarely do you hear people say, "There is a negative family pattern that must be broken." You do that by rising up, taking a stand, and breaking every power.

I'm standing with you; you will give no provision to the flesh. Don't let the devils back in; this is how you do it. You establish a separation. You say, "You know what? I'm walking with God." You tell the devil, "You're not going to want to go here because we're walking on the holy sapphire. We're going to walk in holiness and pray in tongues." The devil won't like it; this is where you part ways with him and push him away. You say, "You know, I'm not giving in to you anymore. God loves me, and I'm going to walk with God now."

The generational curses and evil problems in your life all concern the flesh.

Don't give any provision to the flesh, and that will create the separation as you walk with God. You wonder, "Why did I put up with this all my life? Looking back, it was vital for me to understand why I was even accepting and putting up with this, and this will happen to you too.

That's why you don't hear me praying like this often over people. I educate people that they need permanent freedom, so the demons don't come back and bring more devils. I'm tired of seeing people get free and then bound again. It's because they didn't understand the workings of the Spirit. You must shut these doors and say no. It's as easy as walking away and not doing what the devil wants you to do.

People are not getting their breakthroughs because they are having problems and can't hear from God. People will tell me, "I can't hear from God, but the devil told me this yesterday." So people can hear the devil and quote him, yet they don't know what God is saying to them.

Let me help you by putting a new perspective on how to look at this. How often has the devil told you that you are not worth anything? Well, that's what God is saying to the devil: He is worthless. Therefore, the devil is projecting onto you what he is. The devil is not worth anything. He's finished, and he's already judged. Jesus said the prince of this world has already been judged. The next time the devil tries to make you feel worthless, remember he is the one that is worthless. Resist the devil and his lies. Let's pray and break the generational spirits right now.

PRAYER:

Father, in the name of Jesus, I stand before You with the full authority given to me by my Lord and Savior. You sent Your Son to shed His blood. That blood is so powerful, and the name of Jesus is above all names. I invoke the blood of Jesus and that name above all names, Jesus Christ. I break every generational curse and spirit over all my friends worldwide in the name of Jesus. I break those powers. I pray, Father, that all my friends would say no to the flesh and worldly possessions right now. Father, we are partakers of the divine nature and escape corruption in the world caused by lust. We give no provision to the flesh in the name of Jesus, and all those familiar spirits and curses are broken right now. You lie, generational devils. Yes, it stops now. In Jesus's name. Amen.

What did the Holy Spirit show you while reading/praying through this question:

How can you do deliverance on yourself?

Christians should be in less bondage than they are. Many are still bound because of victimization, trauma, and the spirit of rejection. These issues bombard people for years. You may need to talk about it with others or confess past sins. Talking about it can begin that healing process.

Ultimately, it's better to have someone else pray who walks in dominion and authority and doesn't have the same issues going on in their life. They might have overcome the same issue by themselves, or it's just not specifically a problem for them.

I would have a group of believers pray over you. Commit yourself to a group of people you can trust, let them pray over you, and then deal with the issues that come up. There is a cycle that needs to be broken. Unresolved trauma allows the devil to be there. If you're having problems, bad dreams, and all kinds of temptations, you can break the devil and the tormentors. You can get a friend to agree with you and pray for you.

Find a great church. The local church can help and support you so that you can escape this spiritual entrenchment. Ask a facilitator, the leader, if you could get prayer. Sometimes a group of people might be required as the evil spirits can be stubborn, and with a group of Spirit-filled believers, the devil will be pushed out.

There are different levels of demons, and certain devils are very stubborn. They are aware of whether you understand their place and command them to go or if you are not sure of your authority.

An analogy we can picture in the natural is how horses react. When a horse is with their owner, they learn to behave. They wouldn't get their snacks or grain if they did not act as the owner desires. When we would ride horses in other places, horses that were not our own, those horses didn't know us, and we didn't know them. Therefore, they always try to push their limits because they think, *Well, maybe I can do this to this rider and get away with it.*

With a new horse, you must first be stern to establish your authority. The same thing happens in the spirit realm. You must show your power; these demons know your name and actions because they talk to each other. If you know who you are, you know your authority, and you've cast devils out, it gets around that you cast out demons.

I had my friend Nick pray for me once because he has seen so much deliverance personally and in others' lives. At one time, he was clinically diagnosed with schizophrenia. The doctors had signed the document, and once it was signed, there was no going back; it was final. A diagnosis cannot be taken back. After the diagnosis of schizophrenia, he had a deliverance where these entities left, and he was completely cured. According to the world, it was incurable. Now, he has a document diagnosing him as clinically schizophrenic; even though he is in his right mind, he cannot get the diagnosis reversed.

He ended up working at that facility that had given him the diagnosis. He told us he had twenty-five nurses under his leadership and would sit at weekly staff meetings with the doctors who had diagnosed him with incurable schizophrenia. He was a total miracle and a testimony to those doctors.

I had him pray for me, and for three months after that, I didn't have one peep out of a devil or anyone else. I didn't see any manifestations in people at all. The devil just left me alone strictly because this guy prayed for me.

While I was working at the airline, people often manifested. I handled and interacted with anywhere from six to nine hundred people daily. I said hi and goodbye and took care of that many people on five different flights. I handled all kinds of paperwork and situations. Sometimes, we had to call the police, and people would be hauled off. All these situations were because of manifestations no one knew about in the physical realm. I didn't tell the cops it was a devil or anything. People were arrested because they had spirits in them.

After Nick prayed for me, I had no problems for three months. That was like a record! There was not one incident while I continued to work with hundreds of people a day. This is why I'm recommending that the church you attend have people who understand the spirit realm and can help you pray for your deliverance. The devil will not leave you permanently if the church doesn't believe this way. Then you will have a double problem. You must align yourself with a local church that can support you; find a Warrior Notes fellowship in your area because you can't just ignore the problem or the demons.

If you find yourself doing self-deliverance instead of being prayed over, the first question you should ask yourself is, *what am I doing to leave a door open?*

The biggest hurdle in self-deliverance is determining the access point or the entrance where the trauma occurred. What happened to you has caused you to be in this situation where you need deliverance; you must determine this and process the fact that God did not do this to you. When I talk to some individuals, many will ask, "Why did God let this happen to me?"

Sometimes you grow up trapped in a crisis, but the problem is because of sin. If the generations before you were not godly, terrible things might happen to their children. This is a fallen world. You can't blame God for that. God sent Jesus to redeem us, and those devils must go, and that's the bottom line.

If you're going to do deliverance on yourself, you'll need to be strong and stand up and say, "Listen, I've been forgiven." But without counseling, you can't expect to get over what happened to you as a young child because these events must be revealed so that the light of Jesus can shine and expose the dark places (Ephesians 5:13). People are getting to a place where they can't go on; they are becoming spiritually and physically crippled. This even includes people in ministry. They didn't deal with all the hurt, and now it's coming to the surface, and they need help.

Another important factor in self-deliverance is prayer support. You should reach out to a group of people who can uplift you in spiritual warfare. Let them keep you lifted in prayer. Not only can they help in beating up the devil, but by involving other people, you become accountable to them and let them help you seal the entry access point.

The devil will try to come back, and you must understand this problem. I don't mind doing deliverance on people, but there needs to be no room for him to come back. The problem is getting on the same page with the Word of God so that the devil has no access back into your life.

Victimization happens through rejection or a traumatic event. Through these situations, the devil and his evil foes gain access to your soul, your emotions, and your will. This subject is profound. Many of you have had terrible things happen to you, horrible things. You can't even process what happened, so you need someone else to help sort through the rubble of that terrible event. If you want to do deliverance on yourself, it would be best if you got down to your fighting weight. You need to pick a good day, and you must mean it. Then declare freedom over yourself and tell the devil that this is his last day to harass you. You must mean it!

Then you begin to say, "I repent of my sins. I am forgiven. This [event] is gone. This [event] has been put under the blood of Jesus and can no longer harm me.

I've received my healing from the Lord because I chose to forgive everyone." Forgiveness is probably 80 percent of deliverance. Then you say, "That's it. I'm going to pray in tongues. Devil, go ahead if you want to stay and watch or listen. I have nothing to do with you anymore."

It's incredible. It's a straightforward process. The devil will leave because he won't want to sit there while you pray in tongues. He doesn't want to hear you discuss freedom and deliverance, so you must mean it. I think everyone would agree that the devils know if you mean it. We can show we mean it when we repent, forgive, and then let go of our hurts. I know those hurts are real. These things are why this question is so important and complex, and it isn't easy to cover this topic in such a short book. You can't diminish the difficult seasons and what you went through because of these situations.

Some people never married because of what they have been through as a child. They never participated in society because they were victimized. This is wrong. If you've gone through that type of trauma, it's time for you to get with a body of believers that can love on you and help you walk through to healing. I know it sounds simple, and it is easy to say all you must do is sort it out and process it correctly. The flip side of that coin is that if you can't process

Forgiveness is probably 80 percent of deliverance.

these issues, you can't achieve freedom from oppressive evil spirits. You can't. However, you can't fail if you strive to repent, forgive, and let go. God loves you too much to let you stay in a depressed state of mind.

I strongly recommend you seek help and have others pray for deliverance because some of these hurts are entrenched. When hurts, rejections, and trauma happen at an early age, and when a person lives with them for so long, it's ingrained in them.

I am for the local church, so I encourage you to find someone locally to help you. A word of advice, make sure that the leaders and those praying for your deliverance are in tune with the Spirit and believe the same way as you. If the temperature isn't hot enough for devils to be riled up and stirred up so that they want to leave, then you're probably not going to get deliverance.

For example, Jesus spoke in the synagogue, and a man manifested right there as Jesus was teaching. The Lord asked me, "How long do you think that devil was there and felt comfortable?" The devil did not begin to manifest until Jesus showed up and the temperature got to a point where the devil became uncomfortable. The Lord said, "This is how you must always be." Every Christian must be hot, on fire, so that the devils begin to feel uncomfortable.

If you feel like you can do deliverance on yourself, then do it. If you need help, find someone strong in the Lord, a buddy, and go after whatever might be entrenched. As I said, you must establish your authority.

This authority also extends to animals, because as I mentioned, demons can even dwell in animals. Animals know if you mean business or not. Think about the ferocious dogs that everyone is afraid of. When I walk up to a vicious dog, I look it right in its eyes. I won't look away because I know I win if I get that dog to look away. Now that the dog is under my authority, we can be friends. People are afraid of a dog because they might have a big growl and bark. The dog might show their teeth and has trained people to respond in a certain way. This is what these demons do.

I'm trying my best to get everyone on the same page to have a group of warriors on earth that all agree. We all have the same Christian beliefs and speak and pray according to these beliefs. We're going to see these devils move out and be pushed out in Jesus's name. We have Warrior fellowships and do a Bible study every week. I do the best I can to bring something to you weekly.

Ask the Holy Spirit to direct you to a church or fellowship and ask for prayer with problems you are having with the devil. The problem doesn't go away just because you ignore it. However, if you can find a buddy or a church that believes this way, that would be great. I would feel better about permanent, forever-free deliverance.

PRAYER:

Father, I thank You that You give people wisdom. I pray that people find a group, a body of believers, in churches with a great pastor where they can have support. I thank You, Father, that deliverance has come through Jesus Christ. I thank You, Lord, that everyone here can let go of their hurt. As we do self-deliverance, we ask for Your guidance, wisdom, and direction. We repent, and we're sorry, Lord. We're sorry we blamed You.

Father, we ask that you show us anyone who has hurt us that we still have unforgiveness towards. We lay all of that before you. We thank you Father that in the same way You have forgiven us, we can forgive any and all who have harmed us. We choose to lay down the hurt and offense.

We thank You, Father, that You can help us process these events. There's healing, and there is the power of God. It's driving out fear right now. I break fear in Jesus's name. Hallelujah. Yes. thank You, Lord. Deliverance has come. We break the enemy's powers over traumatic events that happened as a child. Thank You, Lord. We are born-again, Spirit-filled believers. The Lord has delivered us from all evil. I thank You, Lord, that we're releasing our feelings to You. We're opening our emotions to You, Father. We're letting go of hurt right now. I break the power of the enemy. I command every evil spirit, every addictive spirit, every spirit that binds, every familiar spirit, to leave in Jesus's name. Go in Jesus's name. There is so much deliverance right now. Hallelujah.

We're Christians, we're believers. We walk in the freedom Jesus Christ has pronounced over us. He sees us with Him in Heaven. We're far above all evil spirits through our authority, power, and dominion. We break all this evil in Jesus's name. Every addictive spirit goes in Jesus' name, right now.

The Lord is moving so powerfully. All is well. Whatever emotional healing you need, whatever physical healing you need, the anointing is flowing. The Lord is pronouncing you well, healthy, and free in the name of Jesus. You are coming upon a new day filled with God's holy fire. You will be released to drive out every evil spirit, and we thank You for the Holy Spirit that is so strong. The Holy Spirit is overwhelming you right now; you feel the love of God. Let the Father love on you. Right now, deliverance has come.

Father God, help the people understand that the evil spirits love where they inhabit; they do not want you to get this revelation and kick them out. We are taking authority right now and proclaiming that we are coming to take back our rightful place. We are pushing out all the evil. The Spirit of God says I'm coming; I'm coming with power. He who dwells in the secret place of the Most High God shall have no evil come near them. No evil shall dwell where the Spirit of the Lord resides. Thank You, Lord, that the lion is roaring. The lion is booming right now. The Lion of the tribe of Judah is roaring. Hallelujah. Thank you, Lord.

We claim healing for all health issues, including the liver, kidneys, and heart problems, in Jesus's name. Hallelujah. All kinds of financial miracles will happen because the devil has been told to release the believers' finances; economic miracles are coming because the devil is letting go of your finances right now. The Lord has your finances. Hallelujah, hallelujah. Thank You.

My mission in life is to thank You, Father. Thank you, Lord. The prophet Zephaniah says You sing songs of deliverance over us in the name of Jesus. Thank you, Father.

He wants us to be free and to walk this life out in victory. God is powerful with you. Freedom is permanent. Through this prayer, you have received His full blessing and deliverance. In Jesus's name. Amen.

What did the Holy Spirit show you while reading/praying through this question:

____

____

____

____

What does it look like in the spirit when demons attack someone?

Essentially, demons find someone that has somehow been weakened and gang up on them. But I don't want to concentrate on this too much. They set it up to isolate a person, away from everyone and everything. Your life begins to feel dark and depressed, and you can't see past what is happening. Suddenly, you feel hopeless, can't think of anything positive, or feel as if you want to die when you are under a severe attack.

I saw how demons operate, and I don't want to focus on that but on God's deliverance. Isolation is the number one tactic of demons, just like a pack of hyenas surrounds an animal that is alone.

It is vital to be a part of a body, the local assembly, and find a local church. We have Warrior fellowships because we want people to get together and not be isolated. In a demon attack, once a person is alone, the demons begin closing in on them. You can't breathe or see past your hand, and you can't see your future. One act of kindness can take you out of that attack of isolation with an encouraging word, a phone call, a hand on your shoulder, or someone taking you to lunch.

I don't like to be graphic, but a pack of hyenas or coyotes isolates their prey from the flock and surrounds them. We would see that happen on our property and begin throwing rocks and hitting the coyotes to break them up so the animal could escape. Warrior Notes is essentially using the strategy of throwing rocks to break up the pack.

There are different stages of a spiritual attack: oppression, depression, and then possession. The possession has to do with a dominating spirit that is ruling over you. However, as a Christian, you cannot be possessed. Possession is a spirit that will usurp authority over you. We can't even think that the devil could overcome a Christian because we're at a higher level. We've been made in the image of God as ambassadors—we've been restored. We can't imagine that a Christian could be defeated by the enemy because he was already defeated at the cross. He can't win. A Christian is just enforcing that victory, and the devil should be afraid of every Christian.

People turn to their pastor and say, "I need help," but generally, the request is a year late. I discovered this while instructing students in aviation and was almost killed a couple of times because the student asked for help when it was too late in the game. I learned from that because you must know when to take back control of the airplane. It's the same with a pastor and even a father. In every situation, you must know when love says it's time to step in and do something about it. Unfortunately, most Christians wait too long to ask for help. Many Christians have no one to ask for help, which is not healthy. Christians should have a church they can go to for prayer.

Warrior Notes is not here to compete with the local church. We're just providing a way to bear up under a situation, especially in other countries where there isn't a local body. My mission is to be a vessel for people who don't have churches. They can't get together every week, love each other, pray for each other, and have a solid Bible lesson. That's what it looks like in the spirit realm.

A demon targets a person, and you're being watched if you do anything for God. If you're getting hit by the devil, that's because you are standing up and fighting. The devil is not going to bother people after a while. If he has people where he wants them, he goes after the people causing him trouble. The demons don't mess with people who have developed their discernment and character so that they're not seduced. They know that we're not ignorant of his devices. Paul wasn't ignorant, and he said, you aren't either.

We have the wrong idea about what a Christian is, but the devil knows, and he secretly hopes you don't figure it out. If you see somebody who is isolated, if you see one of your friends who has pulled away and they haven't said, "I'm going to spend some time with God," then you need to call them and love on them because they're being targeted. We need to be careful not to allow any of these fellow warriors to be pulled away, dragged away, or be separated from us. Before you know it, people are in a tailspin and need someone to love them.

The demons don't mess with people who have developed their discernment and character so that they're not seduced.

Three or four times in thirty years, while at work on an airplane, men would come in with no luggage or wallet. Their clothes were perfect, like they had pulled the tags off directly from a store. They sat on the plane, did not order anything, and stared and smiled at me. But when they got off, they often said things to me that only I would know. In this way, I knew they were an angel and came to be with me on that particular flight.

One flight was like a circus, and I was waiting for the jugglers, elephants, and unicycles to show up. Yet this man, an angel, sat there and smiled at me the whole time. On the way out, he said, "Kevin, all people want is to be loved." I will never forget that.

Prayer:

Thank You, Lord, for Your protection over our lives. We take our rightful place, have discernment, and plead the blood over our circumstances. We thank You that we can recognize the enemy's attacks and have the tools to put the devil in his rightful place. In Jesus's name. Amen.

What did the Holy Spirit show you while reading/praying through this question:

PART III

Demonic Strategies

> Why does God let the devil loose? Why did He even let him touch people and do the things he does?

We all need saving and deliverance. Some of you need to be delivered from yourself. We don't understand God's way of doing things. He has a will, so He wants things done a certain way. If you want to be like Enoch—a Christian and hang out and walk with Him—it's His way or the highway. "We love Him because He first loved us" (1 John 4:19). Jesus has already said, "I love you," and then He says, "If you love Me, keep My commandments" (John 14:15). He commands us to obey Him if we love Him.

We can find this same command from Moses in the Old Testament. He was told to tell the people to love God, serve Him, and do what He commands so that all these blessings would happen to them. "You shall walk after the Lord your God and fear him and keep his commandments and obey his voice, you shall serve him and hold fast to him" (Deuteronomy 13:4 ESV). However, if you don't do these things, then you will suffer the consequences. Deuteronomy 11:8–28 speaks of blessings and curses. If you obey, you receive God's blessings. If you don't obey, you will experience all these curses.

In the New Testament, God reveals Himself as a loving Father. However, even God disciplines those He loves. "For the Lord disciplines those he loves, and he punishes each one he accepts as his child" (Hebrews 12:6 NLT).

We all need order in our lives and discipline, although it's not fun at the time.

> *As you endure this divine discipline, remember that God is treating you as His own children. Who ever heard of a child who is never disciplined by its father?*
>
> —Hebrews 12:7 NLT

God disciplines those He loves. God gave us a free will. If the devil tells you something, you only have one option: Don't believe the devil and recognize he is a liar. When he tells you something, don't quote him or engage him on his level. You only engage him on *your* level: You are an ambassador.

The problem is we have so much junk in our lives that demons can attach themselves to that and get into our lives and minds. If your past hurts, traumas, and rejection were healed, the devils would leave and not bother you anymore. When we deal with the root issues that opened the door by receiving counseling and allowing people to pray for us, the Lord will fix these wounds, and we will be healed and delivered.

Since God gave us free will, God will not take the devil away. The devil is here on earth and it's established that he is the god of this world, the prince of the power of the air. He is a small *g*, small god, and is in charge of this world.

Why is there so much pain and heartache if God is in charge of this world? Why are babies allowed to be taken out of the womb? If God is in control, then why do these things happen? You can go through all these different evils and see that God is *not* in control. Jesus referred to this when He said the thief has come to kill, steal, and destroy.

> *The thief does not come except to steal, and to kill, and to destroy. I have come that they may have life and that they may have it more abundantly.*
>
> —John 10:10

You test things to see if they are from God or the devil by asking this question: Is there stealing, killing, and destroying, or is there abundant life? If there is more abundant life, then you know it is God because He made a covenant with us in the New Testament. God gave you a free will, and daily, you choose who you will serve. After that, when you deal with the devil, you realize that some issues might need to be taken care of and resolved.

Right off the bat, I want to answer why God allows the devil to do all these things. God has given us a free will, and the devil does not answer to God. If God were in control, there wouldn't be destruction, lying, cheating, and injustice. Sometimes the devil will leave silently; other times, he will not. But either way, he's got to go. We cannot allow the devil to have a landing spot or any access to us.

"Like a flitting sparrow, like a flying swallow, So a curse without cause shall not alight" (Proverbs 26:2). The idea here is that a sparrow will swoop down and flutter, looking for a landing place. A curse without any reason or cause cannot land on you. The way to live your life is to discern if a demon is bothering you and then resolve to cut it off.

When you partake of deliverance, you can be completely free and stay free. I view deliverance as permanent. For deliverance to be permanent, you must create an unfavorable environment for the devil. Jesus said when a demon is cast out, it goes to arid and dry places. They set up their house in you, and then they get cast out. However, they try to return to see if their previous dwelling is available. According to the truth of the Word of God, if the place is not inhabited, when the devil is cast out, he comes back with seven others more wicked than himself, making the person's condition worse than at the beginning. Whatever we do must be so ironclad that the house is now occupied, not just clean and well-dressed, so that the devil has no room to come back.

If you stay in trauma and rejection, the devil will keep reopening that wound.

There are different stages of deliverance and various ways that the demons want to occupy and harass you. They have a system for how to do that, but they look for your weaknesses. The enemy attacks people through trauma and rejection. The enemy won't bother you if you get off that rejection carousel. You must process, deal with, and get healed of the trauma and that cycle of rejection so that you can experience permanent deliverance. If you stay in trauma and rejection, the devil will keep reopening that wound. I'm not saying I'm right about everything, but I saw this on the other side and read about it in the Bible.

When you forbid trauma or rejection to take a hold of you and you have been healed, the devils cannot return and work their strategy on you. God will not eliminate the devil for you. Jesus gave *us* the authority to cast out demons and has equipped you so that you can get rid of the devil.

> *Look, I have given you authority over all the power of the enemy, and you can walk among snakes and scorpions and crush them. Nothing will injure you.*
>
> **—Luke 10:19 NLT**

If you are not going to stand up against the devil, it will be a long brutal fight. You have to stand up to him. These devils will eventually decide you are not worth fighting and find someone weaker. They will look for another target. Therefore, God's not going to take the devil away from you.

Paul prayed that the evil spirit assigned to buffet him would be removed. The Lord wouldn't do it because Paul had been given the authority to deal with it. Whatever was hindering Paul at the end of his life, he was at peace, probably because he was protected in jail. That evil spirit would rile up people and have Paul beaten and imprisoned.

Everyone wonders what Paul's thorn in the flesh was. In 2 Corinthians 12:7, Paul explains the manifestations of that spirit, and he says what happened to him. Everywhere he went, that spirit just came against him in that city. He had all these terrible things happen to him. The Bible doesn't say it was from God but from the devil and a spirit sent to buffet him. Why? Because of his great revelations. Paul had to overcome that evil spirit, that demon. He said that in his weakness, he was made strong.

Prayer:

Thank You, Lord, for our power over the enemy and that nothing by any means shall harm us. We thank You, Lord, for the determination to stand up against the enemy's lies. We praise You and dedicate ourselves to serving You. We acknowledge that our free will has led us to the trials of this world. We claim our authority to take back our rights. In Jesus's name. Amen.

What did the Holy Spirit show you while reading/praying through this question:

____

____

____

____

How do you keep demons out once you are free?

Jesus made the point that when a demon leaves a person, everything is swept clean but unoccupied. You must let your spirit be fed by the Word of God, speaking it out of your mouth, praying, and allowing the Holy Spirit to baptize you and fill you to overflowing. The Word of God is food, food to your Spirit. When you eat the Word of God, it is the bread of Heaven. You are partaking of Scripture where Jesus said, "I am the living bread which came down from heaven" (John 6:51). We grow spiritually when we drink of His Spirit and eat of the bread by acknowledging Jesus in everything we do. When we build ourselves up in the Word, those devils cannot return.

I want to reiterate that I don't want to cast the devil out of somebody unless I can talk to them and disciple them or make sure someone else can disciple them. I also want to ensure they get material to study and encourage them to read the Word and begin a prayer life right away. When people are saved and devils leave them, they need to immediately pray to receive the Holy Spirit, so their spirits are full.

So let me answer the question by sharing some practical steps you can take to keep that spirit away. Once you are free, first and foremost, you need to accept the fact that satan will try to send those devils back. They will be told that they must go back. What happens when a demon is cast out? They don't have a place to stay, and the fight continues. The ongoing battle is their fight over people. You can hear these devils say, "I want them. No, I am already on them." They will look for easy prey and fight over people. Christians are targeted with special assignments against them.

According to Paul, demons constantly attack the world, and most people don't have any way of resisting them. Paul said that you used to be under the power of the princes of this world (Ephesians 2:2). We used to have no power against that spirit, and that's what's happening with Christians. If a demon leaves, you must close the entry point. Knowing where the enemy gains access is crucial. You may want prayer for a particular situation or desire deliverance from a certain problem. So you go to a meeting or speak with your pastor, and if that group or person casts the devil out of you, the devil's power has been broken.

To clarify, Christians cannot be possessed in their spirits, but a demon can influence them. Peter had the wrong thoughts about Jesus's death. Jesus mentioned that He would die, how He would die, how long He would be dead, and when He would be raised from the dead. But Peter spoke against Jesus's death. The devil spoke through Peter, but he wasn't possessed (Matthew 16:23). Jesus identified what Peter said as the very words of satan himself. Peter's mouth was used by satan, and your mouth, your mind, and your will can be used by satan too. The soul part of you (mind, will, and emotions), not your spirit, is open to the demons.

At that very moment, Peter spoke, and yet just the day before, he acknowledged that Jesus was the Son of God. And Jesus said, "Men didn't reveal this. My Father revealed this." Peter was walking around excitedly, saying, "Look at me. I got to prophesy." Then the next day, Jesus shot him down because he said something from his own mind and didn't have the thoughts of God.

You have the ideas of man, the mind of man; this is how spiritual warfare works. The entry point often times is your mind. Peter's entry point was a wrong idea, a wrong belief, which manifested through words. So you can see how we can get hooked on certain attitudes and views by allowing entry through our eyes, ears, or thoughts, affecting our body. These can become addictive. It would help if you admitted to having addictive behavior. When you are filled and flooded and accept the Father's love, then you have no entry point, so the devil cannot entice you and return.

If a particular thought process or feeling comes over you, this is the enemy. It starts with a feeling or a thought. Maybe you feel out of sorts, rejected, or are dwelling on a traumatic event. This will pull you back into a negative cycle or a tailspin, but you must stop that thought process and think about something else. You might think about the beach with white sand and putting on Coppertone lotion. Suddenly, the devil does not affect you. You can rewrite the scene so that you forget what is happening and go about your day. If you don't rewrite your thoughts, the enemy will continue to try to gain access to you.

If you are free, you're free indeed. You need to fill your life with the love of God because it drives out fear, torment, and rejection, and you're no longer a victim. If you're fully loved and have a revelation of God's love, rejection is foreign to you. When you're around certain people, they say that they can't stop a certain

If you don't rewrite your thoughts, the enemy will continue to try to gain access to you.

behavior. They are seduced. For instance, many people might say that they can't stop drinking or can't stop engaging in some other wrong behavior. You might ask them why they do those things because you might think alcohol doesn't even taste good. Their struggle might be with smoking or any manifestation. It may not be a problem for you, but it might be a temptation for that person.

The way to solve this is with the Father's love. Once you feel accepted in the beloved and not rejected, you can rise above that temptation. You will feel like you don't have to give in to that addiction. You will tell them to stop. Yet you might struggle with something else. Maybe you can't give up sugar; you are compulsive and overeat. Somebody else might never eat sugar; to them, it's no big deal. They go and work out instead. You say you would never deal with a certain addiction, but each person struggles to overcome in a certain area. Whatever you need to deal with, seal it up and seal it well. The devil will not be able to come back.

Prayer:

Thank You, Father, that as Christians, we cannot be possessed by the devil. Father, we do acknowledge that we can be influenced by him, like Peter was. Father, we ask that You seal us up by flooding us with Your light and love so that we serve You. We were accepted and adopted into the beloved. Father, we are free because there is freedom where the Spirit of the Lord is. He who the Son sets free is free indeed. Father, I ask You to help us seal up the entry points in our souls so that those devils cannot have any access. Jesus said the evil ones are coming, but they have nothing in me to hook me. Our story frees us up in the name of Jesus. Freedom, freedom, freedom. Set us free right now in Jesus's name, permanently free. Thank You, Father.

What did the Holy Spirit show you while reading/praying through this question:

____

____

____

____

What do demons not want a Christian to know?

What happens when a disembodied spirit cannot return to a body? They've been disembodied; they have no way of expressing themselves in this realm any longer. They know their final destination is the fiery pit of hell where they will be punished and tormented.

> *They began screaming at him, "Why are you interfering with us, Son of God? Have you come here to torture us before God's appointed time?"*
>
> **—Matthew 8:29 NLT**

The demons' first response to Jesus was that they knew who He was and what would happen to them. The second response was that they asked Jesus if He had come to torment them before their time. They were afraid of what was coming and knew they would be punished. They don't want you to know this, but they spouted it off to Jesus.

We take that as an indication that they recognize Jesus as the Son of God. They also said, "Have you come to torment us before our time?" Their time for torment is not now. They have a set time to be tortured. It's coming. The third thing they don't want you to know is they don't want to leave the area where they currently reside. They don't want you to know these things. You need to understand their mentality as you deal with them.

When they are told to leave, they don't go right away. They throw the person down, which is called tearing. They can manifest in various ways, including to the point that it looks like that person is dead. Jesus asked them their name, addressed them, and told them they must go (Mark 5:9-13). They already knew they must leave and that they would be tormented, so they don't want to listen. However, just tell them to leave and that their torment is coming more quickly than they think.

Take care of a devil by recognizing and agreeing with the blood of Jesus. Tell them you were sent by the Lord Jesus Christ, the Son of God, and you have all authority to cast them out now. They don't want you to know that their time has an expiration date. Everything is time-sensitive, and they don't know when the end is coming, but they know it's near. Everything they do is in desperation as they see how many people they can deceive. If they can get a large majority of people to agree with them, a move of satanic activity increases and usurps authority over other people's will.

In government, you see dictators arise, injustice, lying, cheating, and corruption, because the devils entered enough people to get into agreement and push an agenda onto innocent people. If you and your group of believers agreed, a commotion in the Spirit would begin locally and then grow into a movement.

We can do the same thing by driving devils out, and then people would follow godly leadership that would do the right thing, and everything would change immediately. The devils don't want you to know they are on a timeline and have a specific job to do. They don't want you to know that they're around and what they're doing because they are desperate and know their time could end soon. In addition, they're invisible to the physical eye.

> *And I, brethren, could not speak to you as to spiritual people but as to carnal, as to babes in Christ. I fed you with milk and not with solid food; for until now you were not able to receive it, and even now you are still not able; for you are still carnal. For where there are envy, strife, and divisions among you, are you not carnal and behaving like mere men? For when one says, "I am of Paul," and another, "I am of Apollos," are you not carnal?*
>
> **—1 Corinthians 3:1–4**

Build yourself up in the Word and become a mature Christian; get out of diapers, put the bottle away, get some steaks on the grill spiritually, and practice this Scripture.

Paul says that a spiritual man makes judgments about all things, but a spiritual man is not subject to any carnal men's judgment. In 1 Corinthians 2:15–16, he refers to carnal people who don't understand the Spirit of God. Paul said they don't know the Spirit of God, so they cannot make spiritual judgments, but the Corinthians should be under the weightier matters by now. They were still on milk but needed to be on the meat of the Word of God. When you develop your sensitivity, it's like night vision, and you begin to see the movement of a devil and pick it up in your spirit, knowing what's going on.

When a familiar spirit is present, I know when to shut up and not talk anymore, because they will take what you say and go with it. When the devils are operating, you must tell people to serve the Lord, or you are done with the conversation. Otherwise, the person is just wasting my time. You might think that's hard to do, but when dealing with people who agree with the devil, you're putting yourself in harm's way. You must get that person to repent. Sometimes, they don't want to; they want to keep this devil.

Once, while I was working for the airlines, this gentleman had been detained, and before the police arrived, I was casting the out devils. The demons were screaming the whole time as they came out of him. The devils were getting nervous, and I sat there praying in tongues. I then told that person, "I have cast out fourteen demons, and this one demon says he's the head honcho and you want to keep him. Is that true?"

And the guy said, "Yeah." The police came and took him to jail.

I've dealt with spirits on a higher level that I don't mention. They don't want you to know that they are there or how their strategies work. They want you to back off and not keep pushing forward in what God's telling you to do.

Another thing the devil doesn't want you to know is that tongues are effective. You'll have these thoughts so that you feel like you are not even saying anything and question if it's worth it to keep praying because it seems like your prayers are not being answered. In the physical, it will seem as if everything is going crazy. When these thoughts enter your mind, they might get you to back off. But if you believe and say it with your mouth, you will receive it. "And whatever you ask in prayer, you will receive, if you have faith" (Matthew 21:22 ESV).

When you speak to your mountain, pray from a place of leverage that the devil hopes you don't know that you have. The devil doesn't want you to know he's nervous when you wake up. He doesn't want you to know that the demons are asking what they will do today. The demons say, "I hope he's not going to buy people's meals for them and love on them." Everything you do as a Christian is effective, but the enemy doesn't want you to know that.

The devil doesn't want you to know that God made this earth for His people and that no one that serves the devil will get anything. If you serve the devil, your reward will be eternal hell. However, if you serve God, your reward will be an entrance into Heaven because you believe in Jesus Christ. Psalm 84:11 says that God will not withhold any good thing from those who walk uprightly.

God gave this earth to His children with all the benefits, but the devil doesn't want you to know that. While we're down here, even though it's a broken world, you can walk on earth and receive God's favor. God wants to give you the kingdom, provide you with an inheritance, and for you to walk in faith. But a spirit is working against these things so that people don't pray in tongues or speak to their mountains to be removed.

I firmly believe that the children of God should be well taken care of. The devil doesn't want you to know that this whole earth was made for man and woman. The Trinity made the earth and people and placed them here. God's intention from the beginning was that creation was all for man. Initially, God gave us dominion, but when Adam and Eve fell, they had to leave the garden. The curse was now on the land, and we inherited this problem.

God gave this earth to His children with all the benefits, but the devil doesn't want you to know that.

In Genesis 1:26–28, God told Adam and Eve everything was theirs and they had dominion over it. But they fell. The same covenant was given to Noah in Genesis 9:1, but then the flood occurred. When Noah got off the ark, he was given the same exact wording to take dominion over everything.

All through history, we look at what God did. He always wanted us to step in, be His children, and walk in authority on earth. Everything that was made was made for us. However, people have chosen, for whatever reason, to serve the devil and demons. At some point, you understand that the benefits are only for those who love and obey Him. God will fulfill these beautiful promises as He says in His Word because we love Him. He's going to come live with us.

We all go to work or begin a business to make money. God gave the covenant promises in the New Testament as He did in the Old Testament. Paul said that we have better promises and a better covenant now in the New Testament. You are supposed to have the best job and the best of everything. Why would God give these to the devil's children?

Sometimes as Christians, we need to sit and think about things logically. God is not complicated. He doesn't say that two plus two is sometimes four and sometimes five. It's just four; it's that easy. God gave an incredible old covenant promise so that if you choose this day to serve Him and do what He commands, all these beautiful things will happen to you (Joshua 24:15). Why would it be any worse in the New Testament?

The Old Testament tells us about healing. Exodus 23:25 says that the Lord will take sickness away from the midst of you. There was no sickness for the children of Israel, their shoes didn't wear out, and they had supernatural water and food for forty years. That's better than any stimulus check you receive now.

We have the new covenant, yet people live off government cheese and food stamps. The devil doesn't want Christians to know that everything was made for them. If you're standing in a line and God has a job for you, then you deserve to have that job before anyone who's not serving God. That's how I got my job.

As I was standing in line, I thought there was no way I would get the job. Nine hundred seventy people showed up for the job, and thirty-three of us were hired. I was hired that day because I said, "Lord, I have served You all my life. I walked away from everything, and You told me this is my job. So today, I'm just going to do this interview because I believe this is my job. If you tell me that I'm going to have this job, then this job's mine." Other people have their stories, but my story was that I walked with the Lord all those years before I got that job.

When a Christian finds a dime in the church parking lot and puts it in their pocket, the devil gets mad. He doesn't want a Christian to have any money at all. Most importantly, the demons don't want you to know they must go if you tell them to leave.

All those things that devils are holding you back from right now must be restored. In the Old Testament, the people did sieges, blocking off the food and water supply coming into the city to starve the citizens so they would surrender. These types of sieges happened in Masada, Jerusalem, Samaria, and other places (2 Kings 18-19; 24-25). In the same way, demons hold sieges; they want to shut down access to your health, finances, and relationships and continue to remind you of your past. These demons don't want you to know that those devils must go if you tell them to leave and a group of believers gets together to pray for you. What will begin to happen is restoration will occur. The back wages are restored, and your health returns.

In some cases, devils stopped the supply line from reaching me because I permitted it. Unfortunately, I didn't know what was happening because I wasn't exercising my authority. You must see that God's a good God and He's not doing these terrible things to you.

The blood of Jesus is speaking. Hebrews 12:24 says that the blood of Jesus speaks on our behalf. It says He is "at the right hand of God, who indeed is interceding for us" (Romans 8:34). Jesus is leaning to His left, whispering in the Father's ear. "Listen, I have [insert your name], so do whatever You said and fulfill Your promises in their life. Send some angels to help them. They've given their life to the purpose of the kingdom."

The other thing the demons don't want Christians to know is that there is a roadmap and a way out of every problem (1 Corinthians 10:13). God could show you something about your diet, and tomorrow, your problem could totally be gone because you obeyed the Lord and stopped when He told you to. Or you did what the Lord instructed you to do, which could change a situation, although you don't realize it.

The Lord has done that for my wife and me. We would go to the doctor, who would tell us we have this illness. We would pray in tongues over the situation, obey what we heard the Lord saying, and go to a follow-up appointment. The doctor would say, "I don't know what to say. Whatever it was, you don't have it anymore."

I asked, "What does that mean?"

He said, "You had something but no longer have it. What I thought it was, it was not."

I said, "So it wasn't this disease?"

The doctor replied, "I don't know what happened, but it's not there anymore." We've had this happen many times. When we prayed, the Lord began speaking to us about a pathway to our healing, and we went in that direction.

Because of the environment on the airplane and going to various areas where the climate was different, my immune system was irritated and weakened. The devil doesn't want you to know there is a solution and a pathway out of every problem. As we mentioned before, Paul told the Corinthians that any temptation that overcomes a person, that presents itself to a person, God will prevent or deliver them or provide a way of escape so they can bear up under it. These are just a few examples.

The demons don't want you to know your rights and privileges; they don't want you to know that you have a better covenant. They don't want you to know that God is working through you in every situation and interceding for you.

Every day, when I pray to the Father in Jesus's name, I see Jesus on the throne whispering to the Father about me. And I see the angels, and they give me hope. The angels say, "I get assigned to Kevin today because he gets it." The Lord told me that there is a list of those who get it. I want to be on that list. One time, an angel said, "We love to be assigned to you because you get it. You're always moving with the Lord. You're doing it. You're not freezing up."

Prayer:

Father, in the name of Jesus, thank You for the spirit of revelation, of seeing and knowing. I thank You, Lord God, that there's deliverance right now. I command every evil spirit to let go of every believer right now. I command that all the wisdom and knowledge of the Holy Spirit flow through them as they begin to see and know, Lord, what You need them to know. The devil fears that if Christians begin to rise, speak to the mountains, and command them, there will be a mighty overturn, a decisive overthrow in the name of Jesus. Thank You, Father, for the Holy Spirit just rising big right now in the name of Jesus. Amen.

What did the Holy Spirit show you while reading/praying through this question:

What is the daily strategy of a demon?

I've never interviewed one, but this is an excellent question. As you are reading the Bible, look at how people act. For example, consider 1 Samuel 13 when Samuel told Saul to wait for him in Gilgal. Clearly, the king was not allowed to do certain things. Samuel was a prophet but also a priest, giving him the right to perform sacrifices. Saul was a king, but he wasn't a priest, so essentially, he was supposed to wait for Samuel to come and perform the sacrifice. Once, Samuel was late by a day. Saul took it upon himself to perform the sacrifice, which he was not allowed to do because Samuel held the office of a prophet and a priest and was in charge of the sacrifice. When Samuel arrived the next day, he was not happy. He asked, "What have you done?"

Saul said, "Well, you know, you were running late, so I performed the sacrifice for you." Saul lost his kingdom over that act because he trespassed into another man's office.

In some Old Testament stories, prophets were told to do certain things, and they didn't do them and ended up dying. Balaam was disobedient, and his donkey spoke to him. He had an angel with a drawn sword ready to kill him (Numbers 22:21-35). In many stories in the Old Testament, men were told what to do, and then they didn't do it.

Let's look at David and his encounter with an evil spirit. When David counted his fighting men, satan is mentioned, because David was told not to count them. He was not to trust in chariots but in the strong arm of the Lord. The command is don't have confidence in your might, in your power, but in the Spirit, says the Lord. David wanted to take a census by counting his men, but that went against what the Lord wanted. The Bible says: "Satan rose up against Israel and caused David to take a census of the people of Israel" (1 Chronicles 21:1 NLT).

The first time the word *satan*, "adversaries," was mentioned besides in the Garden of Eden was in 1 Chronicles.[5] When you read the Bible, you see evil spirits are operating, but they're not mentioned because they're not discerned.

At the time of David, after Goliath, evil spirits and the devil are mentioned. The demon's strategies are to get a person to be disobedient to what they've been told. God gives us instructions; then He tells us, "If you love me, obey my commandments" (John 14:15 NLT). This command is in the Old and New Testament. Jesus would say that all the parables are conditional. The Old and New Testaments are both conditional. In other words, this is what you do, and if you do this, then this will happen. But if you don't do this, this will happen.

5 "H7854. Satan, *Strong's Concordance* (KJV)," Bible Hub.com, accessed February 21, 2024, https://biblehub.com/hebrew/7854.htm.

Conditions are in place because a demon's strategies are to sidetrack you so that you don't arrive at your destination. I'm not just talking about a physical place on the earth but a certain status. I'm talking about mature Christians who are part of the glorious church without spots and wrinkles. Paul said the goal of the fivefold ministry, the purpose and the plan of God, is to build up the body into maturity and unity of the faith. We become purely mature when we're made perfect in love. If we don't have that revelation, we will never get to the place of that maturity.

Therefore, the devil's strategies are to keep you out of the love of God. The devil prevents you from praying in tongues and building yourself up in faith and even greater than faith, which is the love of God. There's faith, hope, and love; the greatest of these is not faith but love (1 Corinthians 13:13). The goal of praying in tongues is to make you perfect in love. Becoming perfect in love and finding unity one with another means you would die on the cross like Jesus.

Jesus said, "Don't hold this against them because they don't know what they're doing." You cannot explain that unless you've experienced it. These demonic strategies are to get you off track because you're going somewhere. In the journey of fulfilling your books, you will also face character training and development.

When you pass away, no matter where you are on the earth, what will matter is did you have perfect love?

> **The devil's strategies are to keep you out of the love of God.**

Did you mature so that your character could do the right thing? Love is not just a feeling where you're emotional, but this love, in its purest form, is discipline. It's like saying, "I will not compromise because I love you. I'm not going to compromise because if I compromise, then you will compromise. But if I stand firm, then you'll stand firm."

Leaders don't compromise or back off because they're leaders; they're held accountable. They're setting a standard. Because of love, God disciplines those He loves and He's a good Father. In Hebrews, the author says that it's not fun at the time to experience discipline. When I obeyed my dad, I didn't need to be disciplined because I did what he told me to do.

The children of Israel were punished because of their disobedience. Moses and Saul didn't do what God required either. The same principle carries over into the New Testament, where Jesus said, "If you love Me, you'll obey Me." He said, "My Father and I love you and will come and live with you." John 14 and 15 says, "If you do these things, you're one with Us. You can ask what you will, not what you need, what you will, what you desire." Desire is different than need.

According to Paul, all your needs are met according to His riches in glory. Psalm 23 says, "The Lord is my shepherd. I shall not want." Notice it doesn't use the word *need* but *want*. I shall not want for anything. The Father is going to take care of everything. You can see now that the demon will kill, steal, and destroy to take away from what God has already done. Jesus has already defeated all the devils; He's acquired everything you need. He's grabbed it for you.

> *Not that I have already attained, or am already perfected; but I press on, that I may lay hold of that for which Christ has also laid hold of me.*
>
> —**Philippians 3:12**

Above all else, you've got it. The devil will work daily to pull you off track, so you don't acquire what's already yours. I hope this is clear because people don't seem to understand what's happening to them. They feel like they are always being pulled apart and can't stay together. Something is always happening to get a piece of you or to try to own you. People are trying to manipulate you. You might get rid of one problem, and then something else comes up. These things happen because of the fallen world.

But they are also demonically inspired by a strategy. The demons don't want you to get out of debt, be healthy, have strong relationships, or be free of them. The bottom line is to ask yourself if you are afraid of anything because that is an open doorway as an entrance and strategy of the devil. But you are to have a fear of the Lord, which is holy and reverent because He's God and you're not.

Since we love God, we should not have any fear. If I held a conference on fear, we would find that people are not automatically perfected in love because 1 John says that perfect love drives out fear, and you're made perfect in love. Then it says, God is love. So if God is love and God is in you, then fear must go. Love and fear cannot occupy the same place. These are the daily strategies of the devil to get you sidetracked so you won't pray in the Spirit. They don't want you to speak or read the Word of God. You should expect everything you read about in the Bible to happen except for the bad stuff, like Saul's disobedience.

You should expect to experience God's love and be flooded with life, love, light, and revelation like Paul prayed for the believers in Ephesians 1. The devil's party is ruined when we walk in all these blessings. You're not living in a fantasy land; none of this is fantasy.

Everything in the Word of God is true. Jesus was always fixing and taking care of problems. If people were sick, He made them well. He was constantly giving out money because it was a custom for Judas, the treasurer, to give to the poor. Jesus would whisper to him, and he would leave to take care of the poor. And that's what the disciples thought was happening the night that Judas betrayed Jesus. Judas was the treasurer and went to give people money.

You have all these stories in the Bible. I would research and pray in the Spirit, and I gained knowledge about the strategies of demons based on people's behavior or sometimes, where it was exposed. In Job 1, satan asked God about Job. When God allowed the devil to touch Job, God immediately said he was not permitted to kill him. However, four attacks happened in the first chapter of Job.

Two armies from neighboring countries attacked Job and his family, killing his children. The devil can use his strategy so that other people come out, other countries, other pagan nations. Then a tornado and some diseases came on Job. Then his wife cursed God. Satan worked his way in, and the crops were destroyed. Unfortunately, satan can use the weather, enemy armies, disease, and close family members to come against you. Finally, his wife gave up. In the Old Testament, we find the enemy's strategies were permitted. Yet in the New Testament, you have complete authority over these attacks.

I've been a Christian for more than forty years. The devil will push your boundaries if you don't stop him. God can help you seal this up so that the devils can't do these things, because you have authority in Jesus's name over them.

PRAYER:

Father, in the name of Jesus, thank You for this wisdom and revelation. We know we are not ignorant of the devil's devices. Father, You can reveal these things to us through Your Spirit and Your work. Father, You can give us strategies to come against the enemy. We know what his devices are; we know how he works. We thank You, Lord, that everything hidden will be revealed in the name of Jesus. Perfect love drives out fear, and fear has to do with torment. We ask that Your love, Father, would cascade upon us like a waterfall. We ask for Your love, Father, as deliverance comes, a revelation of Your love. Hallelujah, in the name of Jesus. Amen.

What did the Holy Spirit show you while reading/praying through this question:

What legal rights do demons have?

At times, a demon has legal rights to be there, and at other times, they're trespassers. A trespasser doesn't have a legal right to be there. A lot of misconception and jargon is confusing, and I want to clarify this, but you will need to look at the question differently.

If you have property, like your house and yard, and post a No Trespassing sign, you have a legal right to protect that property, even using force. Because you've posted a sign that this is private property, you can protect that property, which means nobody can go on that property. At the same time, if you don't post a No Trespassing sign, it is still your property, but then a person might walk across your yard.

Now, if someone knows you and has a relationship with you, that's different. However, if someone wants to come in and usurp authority, to challenge you on whether it is your property, yard, or garage, then you have every right to call the police and have them enforce your rights if you don't want to do it yourself.

At times, the devil passes by and doesn't have any legal right to be there, but when you tell him to leave, he belligerently looks at you. I'm never surprised when he doesn't listen or ignores me the first time, so I will pull up my sleeves and get ready for a knockdown, drag-out fight.

Next, you have a legal right; the demons do not. If you invite someone into your house or to sit outside on your porch, then that changes everything. Even if you have an altercation, the police will want to know, did they break in forcefully, or did you invite them? The same is true in the spirit realm. If you invite that demon in, then you must remove him. If you invite the enemy in, then you've opened your doors so that he can infiltrate your property.

In a court case, a witness will be called on to testify and state what they saw. The attorneys think they will support their client. You've seen this happen. That witness will turn on the stand and say, "I didn't see that, and neither did this person." The lawyer brought that person in to support his client, but that person is either antagonistic or speaking against the testimony. If the person turns rogue and argues with the lawyer, they are declared a hostile witness. Once that happens, the attorney severs his relationship with that witness.

If you let the devil have access into your life, you must repent, turn around, and declare him a hostile witness. You must renounce the sin that allowed the devil access. You must tell the devil, "You have no legal right to be here anymore." The devil

If you invite the enemy in, then you've opened your doors so that he can infiltrate your property.

will try to tell you that you invited him in. But you must be adamant and tell the devil that he is not welcome anymore. Speak these words with your mouth: "You leave now in the name of Jesus." Command the devil to leave.

Imagine if the devil were a physical person, and you must now tell that person to go or you will call the police. You called in the report, and you flipped the outcome. When you deal with demons, find out why they are there. The person has often invited them in, and the devil will tell you they have a legal right to be there. The demon will say, "They want me here."

Then you must work with that person and ask them if they will renounce the devil. I'll ask people, "Are you renouncing the devil? Are you going to leave witchcraft? Are you going to turn yourself over to the Lord?" They must agree and renounce the devil because then the devil begins coming out, and they will not have much more deliverance to do. The devil comes out because you've pulled the papers on them.

That answers the question regarding how we deal with devils. Either they're trespassing or have a legal right to be there, and you must get that person to declare them hostile. If you can do that, then the demons leave very quickly. When dealing with an individual with demonic problems, the first thing to do is to address whether they have sin in their life. If they have unconfessed sin, they need to repent and turn from their evil ways to receive deliverance. You need to tell them that God is a good God and He loves them. Then that devil loses his papers right then and there.

PRAYER:

We thank You, Lord, that we, as Your children, have all the legal rights. We thank You for our power through the blood of Jesus. And we are thankful for the Word of God, which enables us to overcome the enemy's schemes. We praise You and thank You, Father, in Jesus's name. Amen.

What did the Holy Spirit show you while reading/praying through this question:

How do we get rid of spirits that are in homes and property?

You can do many, many different things to get rid of spirits in homes and property. To keep it simple, it all concerns authority and dominion. If it's your house and you're living there, whether you are paying rent or you own your home, you have the sole authority, and a devil cannot be in your house. You think it can't be that easy, but it is.

However, think of it this way. When you take this to a judge, you will present your case and say, "This person is in my house, and he's got a room."

The judge will ask, "Do you know this person's name? How did he get into your house?"

Your response is, "Well, I always leave my door open. I just came home one day, and the person was there and they won't leave." Because of negligence, that person was able to get in, but you have full authority to throw them out. I wouldn't even wait for the judge. I would take them by the neck and drag them out. You might accidentally bump his head on the door on the way out to remind them that maybe they shouldn't enter again.

> **You must tell them that they're not welcome in your home anymore and drive them out.**

What I'm saying is that you must be rough with the devil. In the first place, you shouldn't have let them in, but if you talk to a judge, you can get them evicted. Still, it should have never come to that.

These are two different scenarios if you're in a house, whether you acquired or purchased the home or had one built. In homes we have bought that had previous owners, sometimes it took two or three years to get rid of manifestations there. I'm not proud to say it took that long; it shouldn't have taken that long. My wife and I would sometimes stay up all night to pray, and we would still have manifestations happen. We would push them out. Finally, we had to tell them, "Listen, the person who lived here before does not live here anymore, and you have no authority to be here." We've had the same problem whenever we've purchased a home that had a previous owner. Some evil spirits thought it was their place; this is the truth and probably shocking to many people, but we've got to help people.

If something's happening in your house, if you live there and you're the sole authority, then it's got to stop. It's got to stop! You must tell them that they're not welcome in your home anymore and drive them out. Rid your homes of these spirits. You have a legal right to be on that property.

Devils do not have a legal right to be on your property unless you have given them access to you or your property. Walk through your house and begin to pray in the Spirit; take oil and anoint doorposts. Kathi and I did this in our own homes. We eventually noticed certain spots where we would feel like we were walking through a person standing there, and we would need to break that power.

We have Scripture and teachings playing all the time, and they don't like that. They end up packing up and leaving because they don't want to listen to the preaching of the Word of God all day and night. We played these twenty-four hours a day.

You need to take authority over evil spirits; they think they have legal rights because someone else allowed them to be there before you moved in and they continue to hang out. One time, we had to talk to one before he would leave. I showed him my house; I showed him the deed. I said, "We own this house. This is my name. The doctor that lived here before does not live here anymore. I don't want to see you again." We never saw him again. Before this prayer, you could hear him walking through the house at night, and I could see him.

Somebody needs to talk about this because if you say you don't believe this happens, maybe you need to reconsider. Because, to me, deliverance is permanent, and I will never see this devil again. I will never hear a peep from him again when I tell him to leave and not return because I'm a Christian and a believer.

When we've built homes, we've never had devil problems. No one else lived there, and it was solely ours. That should tell you something. I have not known anyone who has a brand-new house with a devil problem.

PRAYER:

Father, in the name of Jesus, thank You so much for the property and houses of blood-washed believers in Jesus Christ. We take authority over homes and properties. We break the power of the enemy, in Jesus's name, over every person's property. Devils are being brought up now. Hallelujah, Father. Thank You. We drive you out in Jesus's name, and you leave the people's property now. We break the power by the blood of Jesus, in the name of Jesus. Hallelujah. Amen.

Now, walk around your house and pray in the Spirit. Bless the Lord and worship God. Anoint your home and thank God for your house and your property. Thank Him for your dwelling place. Stand against the enemy and stand for truth. Those devils will weaken and leave eventually. I believe that will happen. We prayed that prayer. I felt the deliverance.

What did the Holy Spirit show you while reading/praying through this question:

____

____

____

____

Closing Discussion

This book has focused on how we can be *Forever Free* from demonic strongholds, hindrances, problems with satanic activity, and witchcraft. We're breaking oaths and covenants. We are breaking those lies of the devil in your life. The Lord sets people free (John 8:36). "Wherever the Spirit of the Lord is, there is freedom" (2 Corinthians 3:17 NLT). There is freedom right now for you. Declare what the Bible says with us in the Spirit: We are one in the Spirit (1 Corinthians 6:17). We will see miracles and deliverance happen.

Jesus Christ came in the flesh and defeated the devil, and satan was driven out. Your deliverance is sure because of the work done on the cross. Feel that freedom right now. It is time for these truths to be known, for Christians to know the truth and experience permanent deliverance.

If you are going to break these oaths and covenants that you have made previously, you can do that by repenting and saying the following: "I break all unholy and ungodly covenants. I break the oaths and come against any satanic activity with those oaths." The devil cannot honor those oaths anymore because Jesus Christ has set you free.

When you became born again by the Spirit of God, everything in your past became old and passed away, and everything has become new. When you come against these previous oaths, you break open these covenants through reinforcing and reaffirming to the devil, these satanic spirits, that you have left. Those oaths are now null and void, and those covenants are broken because Jesus Christ freed you.

When you notify those evil spirits, they can no longer enforce that old satanic covenant you made. He cannot impose those oaths against you anymore. Evil spirits are sent to execute a curse and enforce these satanic oaths. When you repent and give yourself to the Lord, curses and oaths are broken because of the blood of Jesus. You're in a new covenant with the Lord. You need to reinforce your freedom in Jesus by verbally breaking those covenants from your past. Any oath you've taken, even the cutting of your body, any commitment you've made, you have to verbally repent of those and then tell those devils they can no longer operate and enforce that curse.

The Holy Spirit and the angels enforce blessing; they're working for the kingdom, and the Holy Spirit is inside you. He's working with God to bring you to perfect maturity. He is your Comforter, Counselor, and enforcer of the blessing. The Holy Spirit is inside you, enforcing the covenant that overrides any previous agreements. Those devils must be forcefully removed, and you must be rude to them. You must be violent and say, "Listen, you're done, and I'm not listening to you. You have no power over me. Those covenants are broken in the name of Jesus."

Some of you have opened yourself up to the demonic through witchcraft. You have taken oaths, and those are broken in the name of Jesus. You must tell those evil spirits they no longer have a legal right over you because the blood of Jesus is more powerful than any oath you have ever taken. Your pledge to God, your covenant with Him, is the greatest. If you tell those devils they must leave, you must remove any reminder of those from your home.

And this is why it's not good to have certain items in your home that would remind you of the past or any idol, anything from a previous religion. It would be best to eliminate those because they no longer belong to you. Demonic spirits sometimes identify with those artifacts, and they think they have a legal right to come into your house. When you break those oaths, remove anything from your life that reminds you of your past. The Lord will guide and lead you. I'm not going to tell you what those items are, but the Lord will speak to you about all that.

Most people struggle with knowing the difference between waiting on God and what He has for you and the fact that demons might be holding you back or even stopping you. People do not invest in their spiritual life. It is not going to cut it when you have one cold spiritual snack a week in church while feeding your soul three hot meals a day of worldly food. As believers, we have discernment to know and discern between good and evil. The gift of discerning spirits is given as the Spirit wills. However, to be a warrior and stand firm in what God has for you, you must feed your spirit. You develop and gain sensitivity in discernment by praying in the Spirit and meditating on the Word of God. These actions create a wise person, and I believe you are wise.

As you grow in sensitivity to the Spirit of God, you will know the difference between being pushed or being held back. We are a sailboat, and God blows into our sails so that we move forward by the Spirit. We are not a power boat that is driven and pushed. Cattle are driven. However, sheep are not driven but led. We are guided by the Spirit of God and are God's children. The Spirit of God leads us. "For as many as are led by the Spirit of God, these are sons of God" (Romans 8:14).

When you sense in your spirit that a demonic entity is holding you back, then you must take authority and break the enemy's power. Daily, I go before the Lord in prayer to discern and get a release as to what is happening. You may recognize that a demonic spirit is preventing you from advancing and having that breakthrough. Other times, you will know that you are supposed to wait on God, because it isn't the right timing. Discovering the right timing will take wisdom.

When I discern a hinderance in my progress, I find the devil and go after him. I bind the devil and command him to go. Then, if I feel the release to move forward and to act, I continue to do that. If I feel the Lord giving me peace and say, "Just rest and wait on me," then I know it's not time yet. God is in your spirit, and your spirit leads and directs you. Your head or body does not teach you the things of the spirit. You'll know if the devil is holding you back or if the Lord is saying, "Listen, rest in peace, and wait on Me."

We believe in God for miracles and deliverance; we believe in God for intervention in every area of our lives, including financial, health in our bodies, and relationships. We believe that mental illness must go in Jesus's name. Everything is complete. We're asking God to move by His Spirit.

Prayer:

We yield to You, Father. We thank You, Father, so much for everything You are doing. Thank You, Lord God, that we can agree to touch any one thing together. If we believe and agree, we shall receive what we've asked for in prayer. Father, we stand with You and thank You for Your covenant with Jesus Christ, Your Son. We thank You for the blood covenant. We thank You for Your power that raised Jesus from the dead. That same power is dwelling in us. Thank You, Lord God, for deliverance. Thank You that every demonic entity has been put on notice; they must vacate and go in Jesus's name.

I thank You, Lord God, that You'll move by Your Spirit, and You will confirm Your Word with signs and wonders following in the name of Jesus. The move of God and of deliverance has begun; healing has already started. Father, I thank You that we are moving in wisdom and revelation, and we're receiving insight into the deep mysteries of Your Spirit. I thank You for it.

In the name of Jesus, we put those devils on notice right now. You must go in Jesus's name as Jesus made a show of you openly, and He has defeated and destroyed you. By the blood, the resurrection, and in the name of Jesus, we command all evil spirits to go. We cast out fear and trauma. Any deceiving, lying devil, we tell you that you must go in Jesus's name.

Holy Father, we need Your fire to consume us; we repent of our sins. We repent for the sins of our nation. We repent, Father, for the lukewarmness of the church; we stand, Lord, in Your fire. We walk in repentance, obedience, and pleasing You because of Your Son, Jesus.

For those encountering oppression and depression, we break those strongholds in the name of Jesus. We thank You, Father, for balancing all the body's chemicals, adrenals, and hormones. The body is coming to normal levels in the name of Jesus. Every demonic influence is broken in Jesus's name. We believe in healing: healing in your heart and soul. We break off whatever may be causing this depression, this oppression. We break the powers of the devil. We ask the Lord to heal your heart, soul, and emotions. We break trauma in the name of Jesus. Amen.

Kathi and I will continue to pray for you to receive your blessing of being *Forever Free*. We began this book with a prayer for the readers to have an open heart and mind, and I will complete this book with that same prayer. May God continue to show you His wisdom and discernment so that you might teach others about God's goodness and His desire for all to be *Forever Free.* God bless!

Salvation Prayer

Lord God,
I confess that I am a sinner.
I confess that I need Your Son, Jesus.
Please forgive me in His name.
Lord Jesus, I believe You
died for me and that
You are alive and listening to me now.
I now turn from my sins and
welcome You into my heart. Come
and take control of my life.
Make me the kind of person
You want me to be.
Now, fill me with Your Holy Spirit,
who will show me how to live for You. I
acknowledge You before men as my Savior
and my Lord. In Jesus's name. Amen.

If you prayed this prayer, please contact us at

info@kevinzadai.com
for more information and materials.

We welcome you to join our network at Warriornotes.tv for access to exclusive programming.

To enroll in our ministry school, go to:
www.Warriornotesschool.com.

Visit **www.KevinZadai.com**
for additional ministry materials.

About Dr. Kevin L. Zadai

Kevin Zadai, PhD, was called to the ministry at the age of ten. He attended Central Bible College in Springfield, Missouri, where he received a Bachelor of Arts in theology. Later, he received training in missions at Rhema Bible College, a ThD from Primus University, and a PhD from Life Christian University. Dr. Kevin L. Zadai is dedicated to training Christians to live and operate in two realms simultaneously—the supernatural and the natural.

At age thirty-one, Kevin met Jesus in Heaven, got a second chance at life, and received a revelation that he could not fail because it is all rigged in our favor! Kevin holds a commercial pilot license and is retired from Southwest Airlines after twenty-nine years as a flight attendant. He is the founder and president of Warrior Notes School of Ministry. He and his lovely wife, Kathi, reside in New Orleans, Louisiana.

WARRIOR NOTES
SCHOOL OF MINISTRY
ENROLL IN DAYS OF HEAVEN ON EARTH AND HEAVENLY VISITATION AT NO COST!
FREE ENROLLMENT
WARRIORNOTESSCHOOL.COM
EARN YOUR ASSOCIATE'S, BACHELOR'S, MASTER'S, OR DOCTORATE DEGREES WITH DR. KEVIN ZADAI!
Associate's
Bachelor's
Master's
Doctorate
WARRIOR NOTES SCHOOL OF MINISTRY IS AN ACCREDITED BIBLE COLLEGE
W
N

NEW TITLES

by Dr. Kevin L. Zadai

Deliverance Made Easy
& Companion Study Guide

Utilizing insights from key biblical texts, including Genesis 6 and Ephesians 6, Dr. Kevin Zadai delves into the roots of demonic influence and reveals the defensive strategies that play a crucial role in your life of complete victory.

Kevin has written over sixty books and
study guides. Please see our website
for a complete list of materials!

www.Kevinzadai.com